soul talk
earth walk

soul talk earth walk

IMAGINE IF YOU COULD HEAR WHAT
YOUR SOUL IS TRYING TO TELL YOU

MEL RYAN

Disclaimer – The material within this book is not intended as medical advice and should not be substituted for the advice of a medical practitioner. Any reader who experiences problems with their health should consult their medical practitioner.

Names of clients within this book have been changed to protect their privacy.

Published by Mel Ryan
www.melryan100percentyou.com

First published 2014
This edition published 2015, reprinted 2022

© 2014 Mel Ryan

The moral right of the author has been asserted.

All rights reserved. Without limiting the rights under copyright restricted above, no part of this publication may be reproduced, stored in or introduced into a retrieval system, or transmitted, in any form or by any means (electronic, mechanical, photocopying, recording or otherwise), without the prior written permission of both the copyright owner and the above publisher of this book.

A catalogue record for this book is available from the National Library of Australia

ISBN: 978 0 9944168 0 3 (pbk)
ISBN: 978 0 9944168 1 0 (ebk–ePub)

Designed and typeset by Helen Christie
Printed by Ingram Spark

*To those of us who believe anything is possible,
no proof is necessary ...
but to those of us who don't believe,
no proof will ever be good enough.*

Believe in yourself and all that you are. Know that there is something inside you that is greater than any obstacle.

CHRISTIAN D LARSON

CONTENTS

Acknowledgements	1
Foreword by Michelle Tetley	3
Why did I write *Soul Talk Earth Walk*?	7
PART ONE – UNDERSTANDING OUR SOUL SELVES	**13**
Learning to understand	15
Understanding our souls	19
Mercury	23
We are souls – we really don't end	27
Soul emotions … Earth emotions	31
Deserted island	35
PART TWO – UNDERSTANDING WHY OUR SOUL SELVES GOT LOST ON EARTH	**39**
Soul purpose, soul history, genetic history, personal history	41
Soul Earth Self	49
Belief systems	57
That lost feeling	63
Ladders	69
Understand our Earth type	75

PART THREE – UNDERSTANDING OUR SOUL LESSONS ON EARTH — 85

Introduction to soul lessons — 87
Beginning to understand — 91
Understanding and embracing lessons — 97
Forgiveness — 103
Themes — 111
Working ourselves out — 117
Hints we are given — 121
Unconditional love — 133

PART FOUR – UNDERSTANDING WHY OUR EARTH SELVES GET LOST ON EARTH — 139

Power bubbles — 141
Soul parent Earth parent — 147
Responsibility — 153
Change — 161
Worrying about things — 165
Trust — 173
Guilt — 181
Removing guilt from your life — 185
Raffle tickets! — 189

PART FIVE – UNDERSTANDING OUR EARTH SELVES ON EARTH — 193

Expectations — 195
Blame — 201
Creating the same pattern — 205
Everything we need — 209
Embrace feelings — 213

Anger	221
Everything is a mirror	225
Clearing feelings	229
Breakdowns	233
Bake your cake!	241
PART SIX – UNDERSTANDING OUR RELATIONSHIPS ON EARTH	**245**
Understanding our reactions to people	247
The real story	251
Communication	259
Rock story	265
Help people understand you	271
Understand them	275
Challenge each other	283
Conclusion	287
Glossary	289
References	293
Affirmations	294

Until you spread your wings

you will have no idea

how far you can fly!

UNKNOWN

ACKNOWLEDGEMENTS

To my mum who is my greatest soul teacher, thank you, I love you with all my heart.

To my dad, thank you for teaching me to listen – it is everything.

To my siblings Shell, Matt and Sim, it is our different perspectives and yet our similarities that started me on this path. Thank you for always being there.

To my husband, who helped me break my rock. Who planted his rose seed with mine, who has been my protection, my strength, and saw my flowers before I could, you are a gift that I will always be in awe of. I have learnt to love me because you are you.

To all my children, Danielle, Nick, Steph and Sam, who inspire me to find me, and constantly teach me to just love and be me. If I can give you anything in life then please let it be the ability to listen to yourselves and to truly love who you really are.

To my beautiful girls, Bec and Dani, thank you for sharing the bigger picture with me. There is a reason for everything.

Blessings, peace in life and love to you all,
xoxoxo.

> *Stop being afraid of what could go wrong and start being positive about what could go right.*
>
> — UNKNOWN

FOREWORD BY MICHELLE TETLEY

Many people wish for a better life. They hope for some kind of miracle or someone to guide them to make their life better and to make their dreams come true. Sometimes they reach for a book which they hope will give them the answers they need.

This book is different.

Rather than searching for solutions outside of ourselves, the author, Mel Ryan, challenges us all to look within ourselves, to listen to ourselves, to become our own best friend, to truly understand ourselves and, in so doing, to realise that **we** have the power to make our life everything we want it to be. She does this, not by claiming to have all the answers, but by challenging convention, listening to her inner self and teaching us how we can do this for ourselves.

Have you ever wondered why things keep happening to you? Why you keep getting sick? Why you keep facing challenges in your life? I certainly have. So has Mel, but, unlike most people, she decided to work out why. Not satisfied with the answer that 'things just happen', Mel has talked to and treated many people through her work in kinesiology.

In this book, Mel details the themes of the journeys

people have shared with her and the understanding that has come from exploring these journeys. She has explored with clients the reasons behind the challenges they face. For each of these people, she has helped them to answer the 'why' and helped them to work out how they can take back their power and learn more about themselves. *Soul Talk Earth Walk* presents the concept of looking at life and yourself in a whole new way.

I have shared much of this journey with Mel, having known her all her life. She is an amazing and insightful lady with a beautiful inner peace, a warm, loving, joyful heart and a fierce determination to help others find their own peace and joy. Like all of us, Mel is learning and seeking to understand life with all its joys and challenges.

You can become who you are meant to be. Listen to your body. Listen to your soul.

Our deepest fear is not that we are inadequate. Our deepest fear is that we are powerful beyond measure.

MARIANNE WILLIAMSON

There is no greater burden that a person carries than the burden of a person's potential.

UNKNOWN

WHY DID I WRITE
SOUL TALK EARTH WALK?

When I was a little girl around the age of four, I remember constantly asking why? I would ask about everything from how nature worked, to why things happened, to why people did what they did. I desperately needed to understand. I always needed more information so I could see the bigger picture. Only when I could work things out in my head, to find what I thought the why was, could I have peace. For a short while. Then I would move on to the next question! I used to drive my parents crazy until my mum's response became, "Because Y is a crooked letter that can't be made straight!" This never deterred me, although it did frustrate me no end. I remember often saying and thinking there was a reason for everything.

When I was 23 I was in hospital after having my first child. She was crying and I was feeling overwhelmed trying to soothe her. A nurse came in and said she does something called kinesiology. At that stage I didn't care what she did as long as she could stop my baby crying. A short time later my daughter was fast asleep on my chest and I felt completely different. She went through and discussed with me what she had discovered through the balance she had done. (In kinesiology, a treatment session is called a balance.)

She helped me understand. She gave me the WHY!

It was one of the most amazing moments of my life. As a result of that balance I never went back to my corporate job in the city. I studied kinesiology, Pranic healing, Chiron healing, nutrition, massage and many other courses over the next four years, devouring everything. The more I studied the more things made sense. Now I could find out WHY!

Many years later, I am still asking WHY. Working with people for 20 years and being a kinesiologist has enabled me to live this and to embrace it.

Every kinesiologist is different. We all work a little differently and we specialise in different things. The thing that we bring into our work that is different is ourselves, our life experience and what is important to us. I am all about the WHY and understanding the WHY.

Now I get to help people understand themselves: why they block themselves; why they attract things and situations into their lives; what their bodies are trying to tell them; why they repeat patterns. The wonderful thing is that what we are really doing in their balance is helping them listen, helping them to be free: free of the limitations they put on themselves; free to love themselves, clients then get to begin the journey of just being them. It has been a privilege and at times an honour to see people understand and embrace who they really are. In fact they have taught me to be able to do the same.

Finding why and what our bodies are trying to tell us is not limited to any age. Clients are everyday people I have worked with: in utero babies, babies, children of all ages and abilities to teenagers, mums, dads, grandparents, doctors, nurses, lawyers, factory workers, tradespeople, professional sports people, teachers, singers, actors, dancers, police, business people and drug addicts. Kinesiology and helping someone understand themselves is not limited to anyone or anything.

A kinesiology session is called a balance. It's called a balance because in every situation we balance their 'being' – their physical, mental, emotional and spiritual bodies. The balance always starts with listening to and understanding that person's perception of the situation. There is no right or wrong. Everyone can only see things their way and can only respond to it with their own emotions. When working with people it is completely irrelevant to me what someone else 'did' because I can only focus on the person before me, their interpretation of the situation, how they feel from that experience, why they got here, how we understand that and how we can understand them because of it.

This means I can have great delight in treating whole families because each person's experience is unique. It's a secret way of them learning to understand themselves. There is no blame.

Most come willingly, but some clients have been dragged in by their mums or partners. Some clients come in saying this is their last hope after trying everything else.

Working with clients, listening to their life stories and using the skills of kinesiology, has enabled me to help people find out their whys. Why they have depression, or why they can't get pregnant, why they feel overwhelmed by responsibilities, why they struggle at school, work or home, why they feel like they don't fit in, why they try something and it just doesn't work, why they keep attracting what they perceive as bad luck into their lives, why they keep repeating the same pattern.

Or why they have a sore foot, kidney problems, backache, headaches, toothache, high blood pressure, asthma, hayfever, snoring, period pain … the list is endless and for every pain there is a WHY!

I was trying to explain kinesiology to an eight-year-old boy, and after a while he said, "So you are an interpreter for my body then?" I answered, "Yes, yes I am!" A very clever boy, sometimes the simplest explanation is the best.

I would often come up with little stories to help get an example across to a client, to help them understand themselves better. I found after seeing clients for so long that we are all the same, we all struggle with the same issues, we all get manipulated by the same words and we can all feel alone in a room full of people.

After many years the things that have been coming up as issues for people have been very similar, issues that really block people from moving forward. Guilt, doing for everyone else, feeling taken for granted, just to name a few. I found that the words and stories I have used as examples to help people embrace who they are and where they are at, have been the same.

I have seen so many people change their lives through beginning to embrace and understand who they are. I get to see them really enjoy their lives and to feel peace. Because of this I am writing down the journeys and discoveries that we have made, for everyone to share and to give everyone an opportunity to love themselves, love their lives and have peace every day.

    Love to all,
    Mel,
    xoxo

Part One
UNDERSTANDING OUR SOUL SELVES

The first step to getting somewhere is to decide that you are not going to stay where you are.

UNKNOWN

LEARNING TO UNDERSTAND

In 20 years of working with clients I have found only one secret in life that unlocks all the doors to living. That secret is to understand. Firstly and most importantly, understand yourself. To understand yourself you need to research. We can find out about ourselves through our response to other people, events and stories.
- Talk to others about their perspective on life
- Read, read, read from books or online
- Research ideas and concepts that interest you
- Listen to what your body is telling you
- Listen to what is going on in your life
- Feel how you respond to things
- Think about what you attract into your life and why
- Learn about new things – take a class
- Don't be afraid to try new things
- Understand who you are from your past
- Take responsibility for your life, past, current and future
- Participate in a workshop.

By doing this you will hear many different opinions and share many people's experiences and their perspective on life. You will hear many convincing stories. Remember, people speak from their own experiences with convincing passion and what is right for someone else may or may not be right for you. Too often we adopt how someone else thinks and feels and we stay lost.

To understand there is one simple rule: *listen*. Then, I invite you to feel and listen to yourself, really feel and think what is right for you, what resonates within your soul, what gives you peace. Just concentrate on yourself, not anyone else's thoughts or views.

Listening to yourself may mean you take only one thought from one book and two thoughts from another, something from this course and a bit of information you heard from someone else, but now you are on your way to discovering who you really are. The more we communicate, listen and feel how we respond to what we hear, see, learn and experience, the more we will discover who we really are. Only then will we feel more peace every day in our life. No matter what happens.

The word listen contains the same letters as the word silent.

ALFRED BRENDEL

To be yourself in a world that is constantly trying to make you something else is the greatest accomplishment.

RALPH WALDO EMERSON

UNDERSTANDING OUR SOULS

I have always asked why and when I was little I use to think everyone else had the answers. As I got older I realised other people's ideas were good but not quite a perfect fit. Even down to being brought up a Catholic, some things were okay, but others didn't fit so well.

I remember when I was in year 11 having an argument with a religion teacher. The basis for my argument was if God was everywhere then why did the Catholic Church only allow us to get married inside a church and not in a garden? Her answer never satisfied me.

It wasn't the first time my questions about religion had left me with a feeling that definitely wasn't peace. It was more a 'why can and do people just accept that as the answer', who makes the rules and what are the rules based on? Are they trying to instil fear in people to manipulate them? Where is the peace? I continued to ask questions about all religions and many other things in my life, and why there were so many rules.

When I started studying kinesiology I was introduced to a huge community full of different ideas, beliefs, religions, and life experiences, it was a smorgasbord of information. I was given books, I listened, I tried other people's ways and

I tried many different courses in things. I was introduced to people who talked about all kinds of things including past lives, karma, and especially that we are here to become enlightened. Concepts that sat okay with me, but didn't completely resonate with my soul.

I still didn't have my WHY.

I have had a reoccurring dream since I was a young child about my nanna and I. The dream was not in this lifetime and in it I was showing someone else what happened to me and where I lived. I was a little girl of about eight years old and I had been orphaned and taken to a little country town in France to be safe. A woman took me in (my nanna – she didn't look like my nanna does now but her energy was the same so I recognised her) and she was concerned about me staying there until she realised that I could speak French fluently. She had a secret passageway with rooms on either side where people were hidden. I was put in a room with a family and a little boy. In this dream I was showing people where I slept and where we had been discovered and where I died. There was no emotion in this dream, just facts. Because of this experience the concept of past lives made a bit of sense to me, but I still wasn't sure.

I particularly liked the concept of 'soul groups' so I investigated further and came up with what feels right for me. A soul group is a group of souls that look after you. There are two different soul groups we each have: a *spirit soul group* and an *earth soul group*.

Your spirit soul group consists of souls, often referred to as 'guides', who are not on Earth at this time but are aware of the stage you are in, in your understanding and they help and guide you through your life, look after you in relation to what you wanted to learn while on Earth, and keep you safe and on track.

Your soul group on Earth consists of souls who are in your life for a reason – to help you learn while you are having an Earth experience. They may be your best friends, children, parents or work colleagues. Sometimes they are people who you meet for the first time and you get a feeling that you have met them before or you feel that you already know them. They help us learn what we need to learn.

What didn't sit well with me was the idea of enlightenment being a solo journey. I would come to Earth, do my lessons, review them and come back again until I achieved enlightenment. The people that I met talked a lot about people being on 'different levels of enlightenment'. This gave me a hierarchy feeling. Lots of phrases like, 'They don't get it because they are a very young soul', didn't sit well with me. In other words it didn't give me peace, so I came up with a theory that does sit well for me. As always, listen to how you feel after you read it. It may or may not be right for you, it is however a very different concept.

Realising how our souls connect — that's the only thing that matters.

EBEN ALEXANDER, MD

MERCURY

When I was in year 2, a teacher spilt a bottle of mercury on the classroom floor. Mercury in this form is not like normal liquid and it split into thousands of droplets that sat on top of the floor. I was asked to clean it up and noticed I could push the mercury across the floor to another ball of mercury and when they touched they would instantly merge into each other to form a bigger ball of mercury. I probably spent an hour gently pushing the mercury together so all the tiny mercury balls eventually formed a big puddle of mercury that we were able to get back into the bottle.

I am like a droplet of mercury taken from my soul group – which is like a larger drop of mercury. When I am formed the droplet of mercury that is me comes from the bigger drop of mercury being my soul group – I have all their memories, all their experiences and life lessons so far! I live my life and then, when I die, I go back to my bigger drop of mercury and merge together adding all my lessons and life experience. So when the next droplet of mercury is formed, it has added my life experience to everyone else's and that will be the basis of their life experience, which is really part of our combined soul group. We are all one.

Eventually when we match another bigger drop of

mercury (soul group) we will merge together forming a larger soul group, and that bigger drop of mercury (soul group) will again match perfectly and join together and form an even larger soul group.

I believe we make up pure love – what people call God, with all of us combined together. Not the God that is the supreme being that sits on a throne God, but the God that is actually just love, or universal energy, a feeling of pure peace. To make this easier to read I will refer to this as God, but feel free to interpret the God word in a way that feels right for you.

When our souls are pure peace we can merge with God. We have the capacity to love unconditionally and have endless peace and joy, we have the capacity to merge with God.

Part of my tiny droplet of mercury is God.

Part of your tiny droplet of mercury is God.

Now we just need to wake up and listen to the part of us that is the tiny droplet that is God! The part of us that is more tuned into the purity of love, the part of us that knows pure peace. We need to rely on it to let us know who we are, we need to listen to it so we can have peace in our lives.

There are no random acts as we are all connected. Jesus, Buddha, Saints, the Dalai Lama, all people we appear to be in awe of throughout history. All of them are no different to us – they have just woken up their droplet more. They tuned into the purity of love more, they relied on it to help them live. They listened to it.

Learn how to see.

Realise that everything connects to everything else.

LEONARDO DA VINCI

We are not human beings having a spiritual experience. We are spiritual beings having an Earth experience.

UNKNOWN

WE ARE SOULS - WE REALLY DON'T END

We come to Earth as spiritual beings who will have an Earth experience. We are not Earth beings having a spiritual experience.

In life it is mostly thought that we are physical beings with a soul, however, we are really souls with a body for a while.

We own our unique identity (soul) before we are born, throughout life and after death.

Definition of death (the Free Dictionary): "Death is the cessation of all vital functions of the body including the heartbeat, brain activity (including the brain stem), and breathing."

Death happens only to our bodies not to our souls.

Right now we are all spiritual beings having an Earth experience. For those of you struggling with any concept of 'the afterlife', I cannot give you faith or give you trust, but I can give you an opportunity:

- to be full of peace – no matter what happens
- to see life from a different perspective
- to trust – no matter what happens
- to understand
- to live like heaven is on Earth.

THE DARK

A story to help understand that we are souls.

People who don't believe.

What happens when they die?

As you perceive, so you believe.

As you believe, so you will receive!

So you don't believe in God – or the afterlife – what happens to you?

So you die and there you are with your thoughts and consciousness in the dark – nothing happens ... and still nothing happens ... and still nothing happens ... and eventually you think to yourself, "Is there more?" ... and there you have it.

HOPE

In that moment of conscious thought of "Is there more?" you allowed your awareness to expand. Once hope is there you have woken up your droplet! Other thoughts now become possible and you have more hope and trust and a connection, which will lead you to your soul group and enable you to continue your journey.

"If we keep our little flame alive, our first feeling of enthusiasm of who we are, without the influence or intervention of others, we will prevail." This quote from Patti Smith I love because it reminds us of just how simple life should be.

PERSONAL EXAMPLE

I had a friend whose little girl Anna had attracted a spirit to her. This spirit was a little girl who would not be convinced to leave and was waking Anna at night, so I did a meditation and found this little spirit girl in a dark room, with old floorboards and no furniture. She was cold and frightened and was surrounded by angels and her spirit soul group, trying to help her but she could neither hear nor see them.

I tried to communicate with her through meditation but there was no connection. She could not talk to me and my presence just made her more frightened. I had the feeling she had died in tragic circumstances, that she felt abused and had not been shown any love in her life. Her experiences on Earth had left her with no ability to trust and no hope.

I left her space and asked the angels for help.

I was given a box – a small square, beautifully-wrapped box with a big bow. I went back and placed the box in the middle of the room and stepped back so she couldn't feel my presence. She was huddled in a ball on the other side of the room. Eventually she looked up and stared at the box for a very long time.

She slowly made her way to the box and turned it over a few times. Finally she opened it. When she did the room became warm, she could see the lights from the angels, she could feel love and she happily left with them. She could not leave before as she had no hope, she had no connection.

Inside the box was hope – the very fact she opened the box proved she had hope.

To remember who you are

you need to forget

who they told you to be.

UNKNOWN

SOUL EMOTIONS ... EARTH EMOTIONS

The beginning of how we get so lost and why it's so hard to listen to our souls.

Before we come to Earth we can experience only free emotions, that is, emotions that can't manipulate us.

Love, peace, calm, joy, determination, courage, strength, tranquility, safety, relaxation, freedom, harmony, hope, being loved, tenderness, delight, awesomeness, trust – all the good ones.

These are our true emotions – the emotions of the soul, they are based on love, they empower us, they are the emotions that we are meant to feel on Earth. The emotions we will always be able to feel because we never stop being a soul.

Then we come to Earth and we discover Earth emotions – trapped emotions – that is emotions that stop you from being you.

Guilt, judgment, inadequacy, unworthiness, abandonment, overlooked, powerless, worthlessness, rejection, lack of trust, incapability, fear, manipulation, loneliness, regret, anguish, doubt, helplessness, feeling unloved, feeling unlovable, feeling trapped. The list is endless. These feelings are the reasons why we stop ourselves from connecting with our true soul self. These emotions are based in fear. These emotions leave us powerless.

Earth emotions can start from the moment we are born, and normally by around two years of age all children are capable of feeling, responding to and changing their behaviour because of Earth emotions. They stop listening to who their soul is, and they will change their behaviour to please people.

INSIDE A SEED

Every seed has inside it all the information to be exactly the plant it is meant to be. Nothing will ever change that. An oak tree will be an oak tree, grass will be grass, a banana tree will bear banana's and a rose bush will make roses. All the information each plant needs even down to the colour of their flower is inside that seed. We are the same. If we imagine our soul as a seed before it's planted (before we come to Earth) all the information for who we want to be need to be and will be is already inside us. Nothing can change the essence of the seed, and to continue the analogy, nothing can change the individual essence of each of us. You can't make a rose seed an oak tree, and you can't make an apple tree a carrot. It's quite simply a fact. Yet we can spend our lifetime trying to be something we are not. We look outside of us to find the answers of who we think we are meant to be.

I speak with a lot of parents who have more than one child. More than once we discuss how can two parents produce completely different children. All their children have the same mother, same father and same environment in their upbringing yet their children are all so different, they struggle and thrive at completely different things.

FAMILY FLOWER BEDS

How can you give birth to children from the same parents that are so completely different?

You get four flower seeds to plant. Each of those four seeds are planted in the same plot. They all get the same amount of sun, the same amount of water and the same nutrients. They grow into beautiful healthy plants budding with flowers. However, when they flower one is blue, one is red, one is yellow and the other one is white. How can they turn out so different? The answer is because no matter what seed we get to plant the colour of that seed is already decided. They will always attract to them what they need to make them the best and most beautiful, blue, red, yellow or white flower. The parents' job is to help them grow, and to understand and listen to themselves and to be in awe of their colourful garden, not to produce the same colour of flowers – that can't happen.

Each of those plants were always going to flower in their colour. Nothing would ever have changed that. Before they were planted their colour was already picked.

Taking time to do nothing often brings everything into perspective.

DOE ZANTAMATA

DESERTED ISLAND

I use this exercise with many of my clients:

Imagine yourself in a place where you are completely alone. No other person will ever be there. It might be a tropical island, a beautiful forest or anywhere else that feels wonderful. (I will use a deserted island for this example.) This is your special place. You are safe, secure, all by yourself. No one else can enter this beautiful place you have created.

Think now, about your ability to love yourself, to completely embrace and love who you are, everything about you, to understand yourself and who your soul wants to be.

It feels pretty good, yes? (Everyone responds to this with a positive muscle response – kinesiology test.)

Now let just one other person into that place, anyone you want, and now imagine your ability to love yourself, to completely embrace and love who your soul wants to be.

Now how does it feel? (Everyone responds to this question with a weak muscle test response – which shows us that there is stress around this topic.)

Now let everyone in – and imagine now your ability to love yourself, to completely embrace and love who your soul wants to be – to love you. (Again everyone responds to this with a weak muscle test.)

Now come back to where you are in life today and imagine your ability to love yourself, to completely embrace and love who your soul wants to be. Now it's even harder.

It changes doesn't it? That feeling of empowerment, freedom and peace that is present with you with the first question – when you can imagine your ability to love and connect with who your soul wants to be – is now completely gone. You are left with a feeling of frustration, lost and overwhelmed. This is how we are experiencing Earth.

You can only feel guilt, judged, inadequate, unworthy, abandoned, overlooked, powerless, worthless, rejected, incapable, fear, manipulated, lonely, regret, anguish, doubt, helpless, unloved, unlovable, and trapped **when you compare yourself to others**. None of these emotions can be felt on a deserted island by yourself. Earth emotions need to be used to help us find out about ourselves, not for us to use them to destroy ourselves.

It is only you who decides which of these emotions you feel when you compare yourself to others. These emotions are self-judgment.

As soon as someone else is on our deserted island we will then, both consciously and subconsciously start to think ... I don't do it the way they do, or think the way they do, or look the way they do, or I am different, something must be wrong with me. It is when we stop listening to ourselves, our soul, that we start to lose ourselves.

Our whole Earth upbringing is based on trying to use earth emotions to find soul emotions. It can't work and leaves us feeling very confused. When making decisions about anything and you can't work out what the correct answer is then put yourself on a deserted island – where you will never see anyone else so you can't feel earth emotions like guilt or trapped – ask yourself the question again. (Some of my clients use this same concept but imagine themselves in a bubble while they decide.) The reason behind this is because your answer will be yours and not dependant on what everyone else thinks. It gives your soul self a chance to answer.

POOL STORY

I have a choice of two different pools that I can swim in. The Soul pool or the Earth pool.

The Soul pool over to my right is a beautiful, warm clear pool surrounded by tropical flowers. It smells so sweet, and from the pool you can see a beautiful sunrise with orange and gold colours that light up the sky. The morning sunlight dances over the flowers floating in the water. This pool contains all the soul emotions – peace, love, joy, wonderment, freedom. All the emotions a soul is meant to feel. I am drawn to it, the only problem is that there is no one in the pool.

The Earth pool is over to my left. It's a concrete pool crowded with people. This is where everyone is. This pool comes with all the Earth feelings – overlooked, unloved, abandoned, guilt, as we have discussed. It doesn't feel very nice, yet I still find myself drawn to it. This must be better, this is where everyone is. There must be something wrong with the other pool.

It is so easy to stop listening to yourself, to stop listening to your soul. To compare yourself to everyone else and find yourself in the concrete pool.

Part 2

UNDERSTANDING WHY OUR SOUL SELVES GOT LOST ON EARTH

Learn to get in touch with the silence within yourself, and know that everything in life has purpose. There are no mistakes, no coincidences, all events are blessings given to us to learn from.

ELIZABETH KUBLER-ROSS

SOUL PURPOSE, SOUL HISTORY, GENETIC HISTORY, PERSONAL HISTORY

So let's begin to work ourselves out.

Too often we never look at our whole past… we don't understand the fact that our soul is always working towards the place that we can be free and truly resonate with who we are meant to be.

Unfortunately, when we come to Earth we get distracted. Our soul life and Earth life become confused. Imagine you are trying to work or study with a huge party going on in the next room and people keep coming in and interrupting.

When we plan to come to Earth our souls are pure, our souls intentions are focused. Then our soul enters a body. Now four things are going on:

1. We have the reason for why our soul is here. What we want to learn here.
2. We have a soul history – memories and experiences of our soul group (mercury theory that we looked at before).
3. We are now in a body – this body has genetic history. Genetic history is made up of two things:
   - DNA makeup – taken from both our parents. All our physical characteristics, including predisposition to illness.

- Emotional patterning. Emotional patterning means that a part of you is linked to your biological parents, which means a part of you, even though it is not a conscious thought, has access to all your past direct genetic relatives and their emotional memories. This can explain why children often seem to repeat the patterns of their parents.
4. We have our own personal Earth life experience to understand (which we will look into in more detail a bit later in the book).

No wonder we get so lost!

Let's look at genetic history in more detail.

The body you now occupy was made by your mum and dad, they were made by their mum and dad and so on – we can trace our genetic history back hundreds of years but it goes back further than this, we did not just appear. So now we are in a body and it is made up of all the genetic influences of the past!

PERSONAL EXAMPLE - GENETIC EMOTIONAL

I can be claustrophobic at times. I hated being pinned down as a child or not having my arms free. I later found out that my dad had suffered polio as a child and the treatment in those days was to tie a child down so they couldn't move! The feeling I had is the same feeling that my dad had; it's an Earth feeling. It has been passed on in my genetic emotional memories. Interestingly my daughter can also feel claustrophobic, and hates being pinned down as well!

CLIENT EXAMPLE - GENETIC PHYSICAL

Working with clients I have found some very interesting things in their genetic past, both physical and emotional. One client had an immune disease that was terminal – heavy metal poisoning that was very suppressed and hidden in his body kept coming up. He couldn't remember a time in his life when he was exposed to large doses of heavy metals. When we traced this back, the 'causal time' of the poisoning came up as conception time for him. His father had worked in a shipping yard as a welder working continuously with heavy metals before his son was even conceived. The toxins from the heavy metals had transferred from the father to the son. This is a great example of physical genetic past.

CLIENT EXAMPLE - GENETIC EMOTIONAL

There is also a huge part of us that is linked emotionally to our parents. Children can manifest physical symptoms that relate to things their parents haven't cleared. A seven-year-old client was having lots of kidney troubles – she had been diagnosed with kidney reflux. While working with her there was great trauma around sexual insecurity but it was very old and very suppressed. After some time I had a chat with her mum. It turns out her mum had been raped at 15 and had never to that day told anyone.

I have also had the privilege of working with genetically-linked Holocaust and Apartheid clients. Even though the client I may be seeing at the time never experienced the direct effects of the Holocaust or Apartheid the emotional link to this experience still remains. The feeling of being trapped, betrayed and powerless, the inability to trust, the anger, goes through all generations.

CLEARING GENERATIONAL EMOTIONAL LINES OR LINKS IN A FAMILY

It is easier to understand this when we can put our Earth emotional responses aside for a moment and look at it from a souls perspective.

Why can babies be born with illnesses or disabilities? Why can children develop a life threatening illness at such a young age? Illness is our soul's way of trying to explain something to us. The fastest and simplest way for our souls to try and communicate with us is through illness. With young babies and children I have found that the issue, or emotional link behind their illness that stops them from getting better quickly, may not just be theirs. They may be clearing things from their spiritual line or their spiritual past – if they had a past life, or if we go with the mercury theory and they are imprinted with past lives, then they are clearing left over Earth emotions. Once you die you can't clear emotions like anger, rejection, guilt and revenge – all the Earth emotions that we have talked about. If you are holding onto a lot of blocking emotions when you die and you hadn't finished working on them, then you may start dealing with these when you or your soul group person (mercury drop) comes back. We are born with soul projects and working on these projects start, from the very beginning of our Earth time here. If a baby is born with kidney issues then they are usually dealing with fear and anxiety emotions. Heart issues are usually forgiveness and self-worth issues. More of what each organ means is explained in more detail later. These emotions will not only be relevant to them now because of the spiritual past they are clearing, but are also relevant to them because of the genetic line they chose to be born into.

These babies and children may also be clearing things in a genetic line. There are some big restricting and blocking emotions in genetic lines. Imagine the genetic line feelings that have been brought back through our ancestors such as from fighting and living through war times, going through depressions, drought, famines, oppression, destitution, epidemics of illness and poverty.

What happens is that the child who is ill is actually giving the whole genetic line an upgrade. They are helping both the past and present souls in their genetic line clear these emotions. I don't know if you have had the privilege of spending time with a very sick or dying child, but in my personal experience and from the accounts of everyone I have talked too or worked with, these children are amazing.

Their strength, their acceptance, their peace and love that they give to others as they go through their illness journey allows their parents and families to see life in a whole new way. Their families get the opportunity to clear trust, fear and anger and find peace and hope through this child. What a beautiful gift for that family!

We actually pick our generational line as a soul in order for us to enhance what we came here to learn. After all, that is why we are here, to learn and understand ourselves. That is why there are so many genetic illnesses.

For example, breast cancer – the women who suffer breast cancer in a family will also be emotionally similar and will all have challenges for themselves regarding nurturing or being nurtured. Diabetes – the people in the family with diabetes will all have a need to control and struggle to feel good about themselves. So it may be a physically genetic illness, however, the person's soul picked that family to help them all learn similar lessons about their soul selves.

I read a story once about a person who could see people's auras. This man was waiting in line at a food shopping centre checkout. As he looked up he could see the beautiful glow and colours of this amazing aura in another checkout line. He was mesmorised and could not help himself but to move to this line to find out what this person looked like. He was imagining a wise older person who had accomplished much self-understanding. When he finally moved to a position to see just who this amazing aura belonged to he was surprised and also delighted. He had learnt something. You see this aurora belonged to a young boy. This boy was what we would say on Earth, suffering many disabilities and would be considered 'special needs'. This boy's aura was magnificent because he was being exactly who his soul wanted to be. He was teaching his family and his community about time, love, care, simple accomplishments and a different way to communicate and to listen.

Your present circumstances don't determine where you go; they merely determine where you start.

NIDO QUBEIN

I've learned ... that our background and circumstances may have influenced who we are, but we are responsible for who we become.

UNKNOWN

SOUL EARTH SELF

Understanding how and why we got lost.

Not only did you choose your family to help you with your soul journey but you also chose your position in the family. Understanding your position in a family plays a large part in understanding ourselves. If you are born first you can have issues with responsibility. You will either take everything on, or nothing. You will either be over-responsible, sorting everything out, or you will avoid responsibility altogether! You find it hard to really take a good look at yourself.

If you are born somewhere in the middle it can depend on what your older sibling has done. If they dropped all responsibility then you will pick it up tenfold. It will be harder for you to fail at anything. Otherwise the middle person can often feel overlooked, that no one takes any notice of them, they are not as important as everyone else, they don't fit in anywhere. You compare yourself to everyone else and struggle to feel good about yourself.

The youngest, especially if there is a big gap, will struggle with making decisions because they have had three, four, five, or more parents (because of older siblings) all telling them what to do. As they get older they are still trying to please everyone. They still ask everyone what they think they should do. They may also feel unempowered, i.e. Everyone else gets things first. It's like I'm not allowed to do stuff or have stuff yet, so I hold myself back.

An only child will either be really bossy, create conflict and struggle with compromise or they will always feel left out, like people deliberately leave them out and may not feel they can properly connect to people. They may struggle with resilience and criticism.

Understand your past, your position in your family, what it taught you, how it helped and how it limited you. Your past gives you an insight into who you are today and why you block yourself. It's not good or bad it's just awareness that will give you an insight into yourself.

Feelings of how we felt as a child will pre-empt how we will feel for the rest of our life. Understanding why you picked that position in your family and what you wanted to feel and learn from your position in the family is the beginning of your journey of understanding you.

CLIENT EXAMPLE
Beth – the youngest of five children came to see me, she was 17, she presented with a theme of not fitting in, not feeling welcome. Her balance focused around 'youngest child syndrome'– always being told what to do and being unable to find her own self-power. She also had a feeling of always being unwelcome as she felt at times like she was 'in the way'.

She came to see me because she was unable to self motivate in year 12. She didn't feel connected to anyone and had continued the not welcome theme in her current situation in her life. During her balance, her not being in 100% present time came up continuously – the time she was locked into came back to birth. Beth was born with her umbilical cord around her neck – she was unable to take her first breath due to her cord constricting her neck – this lead her to start life in a panic-terror state and she remained stuck in shock and trauma. From this time she never felt safe and it had never been cleared. Beth had only been 'here' (experiencing her life) in half capacity due to her fear and her having no trust from the beginning – she had a feeling of 'no power' and 'not belonging'.

UNDERSTANDING THE CLIENT STUDY

Beth had been born and started dealing with the unwelcome feeling straight away. Her decision to be born fifth in a family enhanced her experience of this feeling and she had continued the theme throughout her life so far.

'Clearing this' on a physical, emotional, mental and spiritual level allows her to no longer block herself and her life path with this feeling, but to embrace it and use it to not only understand herself but to be free from it and not keep finding it in her life.

She went on to study effectively, surpassing her expectation in her VCE marks and got into her first preference in university!

CLIENT EXAMPLE

Twins presenting at 37, Aimee and Georgia – Aimee was born first via a caesarian section. Aimee came to watch her sister's session with me. Aimee had recommended that Georgia come to see me.

Georgia, born second, presented with chronic depression, diabetes and symptoms of chronic fatigue. Her whole life she had felt nothing would go right for her. She had in the past attempted suicide.

During her balance, present time came up. She was not properly connected to her time in her life right now. There was shock and trauma around her birth, however the shock and trauma was emotional not physical. We discovered in her plan she was going to be born first. She had engaged in the uterus as the first baby to be born. Her plan was to show her twin Aimee around, to look after Aimee. She wanted to take on the traits of the eldest child – be responsible, take charge. As the birth was an emergency caesarian section the girls weren't ready. Her sister was born first.

UNDERSTANDING THE CLIENT STUDY

Georgia was born in a confused and unempowered state. In her plan she was meant to be born first. She was lost and could not find her place or where she fitted in at all in her life. She felt nothing went right for her because nothing went right for her from the start. Interestingly, having both the twins there they both confirmed this. Aimee was resentful of responsibility. They both said they were always confused by people who always thought Georgia was the eldest.

CLIENT EXAMPLE

Fiona, 57 – had suffered from depression, on and off all her life. Her depression had come back and was quite debilitating, affecting all aspects of her life. Fiona's husband, Glen, had recently gone back to work after not working for two years.

During the balance, self-empowerment came up more than once. In working through the balance, we needed to go back to her childhood. She was the youngest child with two older brothers. There was a gap of nine years between her and the eldest brother, and six years between her and her other brother. She was looked after by everyone in her family. They all had varying opinions as to how she should do things. As a result of this it had left her with a very unempowered feeling about herself especially when around older males. When she was 12 both her brothers had left home and she was left as the only child. This resulted in her feeling of empowerment coming back. However, it's not peaceful empowerment it's conditional, it's empowerment when men are not a strong presence in her life. Her empowerment is still an Earth based emotion.

She had carried this reaction to these feelings right through to her life today. When we looked back on her life we discovered that she had been the most depressed when her husband had been working and their business was thriving. When she felt the most empowered and her depression was absent was when her children 'needed' her (note: all her children were boys), that is, when they were struggling in their lives and she felt she could look after them, and also when her husband was without work and had to rely on her working for their income.

UNDERSTANDING THE BALANCE

Fiona had many contributing factors that led her to being depressed. She did present with all the emotional signs of a 'youngest' child who only found her power at home when everyone left. She carried these belief systems from her childhood through to her adult life. Fiona only feels empowered when others, especially the men in her life, were struggling around her, where she was in a position, like she was when she was 12, of being the only one to do things, and there was no one else to take over.

***

I have worked with many clients who have struggled because of changes in family position. From a death of their older sibling, they have to be both the second born and the eldest. Many clients who are the first-born child struggle with a feeling of being lost and unsure of themselves. Interestingly, when we trace back to when this occurred for them, it can be during their development time in the womb. Many of these clients later find out that they are not the first child. Their mum may have had a baby when she was younger and had adopted them out. Their mum may have had a stillborn child prior to their birth. On more than one occasion I have worked with clients that have always felt like something was missing. When we trace this back to womb time I get them to talk to their mothers about when she was pregnant with them. Most of the time they come back saying that their mum had some bleeding very early on in her pregnancy. This has turned out to be their twin who had not continued their journey to Earth. Everything that happens to us affects us, everything that happens to us can help us understand ourselves.

Instead of giving myself reasons why I can't, I give myself reasons why I can.

UNKNOWN

BELIEF SYSTEMS

We continuously try to hide from the past without embracing it as a part of our journey to help us understand who we truly are.

Between the ages of 0–7 most, if not all of our belief systems that we will continuously refer to unknowingly for the rest of our lives will be created.

A belief system is really an emotional thought pattern that we either create from our own life experience, or we adopt from someone else's, either from listening to what they tell us or from watching TV, movies, reading books. Without us being aware, belief systems influence us every day. We have belief systems because it's our way of trying to understand our environment, our world.

Belief systems may be about things or events, but they will always have emotions attached.

For example, if your mum is scared of spiders, as a child you are more likely to be scared of spiders because you unknowingly adopt your mum's belief system "that spiders are to be feared" when you see a spider.

If your mother died when you were being born and you were then moved to many different foster care homes, it's likely you would develop a belief system of being unable to connect with anyone, with feelings of abandonment or being unlovable.

Religion is about belief systems, self-sabotage is about belief systems: things don't come easily to me, struggling for money, needing to be sick to get attention. Feeling powerless is about belief systems: someone else will make it better, not being strong enough, the list is endless. Each time you experience that belief system you are locking it in again.

Belief systems can be both positive and also hold you back.

Childbirth – there is a village I have read about. The women there give birth and their birthing is actually an orgasmic experience. You see they have never experienced birth any other way so this is normal for them. In the Western world we are exposed to the feelings our mother had when she gave birth to us, we see how birth is portrayed on TV, in books, we have the belief system that birthing hurts through everyone telling us of their birthing stories, we go through birthing classes talking about coping with pain. It would be impossible for us to develop any other belief system around this.

CLIENT EXAMPLE

I had a client who had adopted a baby boy from Vietnam, Joshua. When Joshua came into her care he was 20 months old. Previously, Joshua had lived in an orphanage with many other children. What was most interesting was that he didn't cry when he needed something. You see Joshua had developed a belief system very early on in life. Babies cry to get attention and help. When Joshua cried no one came, so eventually Joshua stopped crying. It was over six months before he would start to use crying as a way to communicate, when slowly he realised someone was there for him.

Every session I have with clients has a belief system involved in some way.

FAIRYTALES

Every culture has fables, fairytales and stories they pass on to the next generation. They can all have an impact on our belief systems.

I will use the Cinderella story as my example. Cinderella was an orphan being raised by a nasty step-mother and a prince came along on his big white horse and saved her, rescued her so she leaves her horrid life and goes with him to his castle and lives happily ever after!

Great story, I loved it as a child. However, I always underestimated the impact these stories could have on our belief systems at such a young age.

For a man, this story gives them the belief system that I have to save someone, to make it better for them, I have to whisk them away on my horse so they can live happily ever after. This belief system adds to the mental space of a man – so providing for a family and trying to make happily ever after happen is impossible. So in lots of ways, men have an underlying feeling of failure.

For a woman, this story gives her a belief system of "I have to wait until someone comes to save me". That getting married is when I will live happily ever after. Women can spend most of their lives waiting for 'the one' to come along.

These belief systems then unconsciously impact on our

thoughts, how we see life and react to it. We add them to our expectations, we block ourselves and we give up our power.

That's why it's very powerful to look back over the little things in our childhood – what stories we liked – because it's just another beautiful insight into our soul selves.

YOUR SOUL MATE

Stories like these extend through to the idea that we have to find our soul mate. Our soul mate is a person whose soul is the same as ours, a perfect match, so to speak. We could become like a pair with them and "live happily ever after". Imagine if your soul mate was here with you, wouldn't it be wonderful? How well would you treat them, look after them, make sure they feel loved and special. How well would they treat you, make sure every need you had was met?

Or here is my concept:

From the minute you are born to the minute you die the only person in your life for every single moment, who has experienced every single experience, who knows everything about you, IS YOU. Think about it for a minute, you are the only one who can do things perfectly for you, who knows exactly what you want, who knows how you like everything. No one else will ever see life the way you do. They can't. They can only see life through their experiences, their perspective and their needs. You are the only one who will ever truly know what you need. You are THE ONLY ONE who can ever really understand you.

YOUR SOUL MATE IS YOU.

Wouldn't it be wonderful if we could all realise this?

A question that I ask my clients, I will now ask you:

If your soul mate was you, would you treat yourself differently?

Go back to imagining your soul mate being someone else for a moment. It's so easy to imagine how you would feel. It's easy to imagine what you would do for them, how you would look after them. Do you treat yourself the way you should be treated? Your soul mate really is you. They are with you forever, they want to help you.

I believe you can meet up with people from your soul group. That is when people say I feel like I have known you all my life. When you meet people and you both just 'click'. You know things about them before they tell you; you have the same interests, and you just love being with them. These are people that are all part of your soul plan. They are all in your life to help your soul understand yourself. These people are soul helpers. Some stay for a little while, but others stay a long time. There is a saying: People come in and out of your life at different times, for different reasons. Let them. Understanding our responses to other people is a perfect way to help us understand ourselves.

If you meet a person who is very warm and compassionate and you love that in them, it's because you have those qualities in yourself but haven't woken them up yet. If they are confident at public speaking or confident in their life, it's the same. We are attracted to people and their qualities because we have them in us and we need to develop them further. Be aware of who inspires you and what you admire in them, because it is a secret hint as to what your soul is working on.

The only person you are destined to become is the person you decide to be.

RALPH WALDO EMERSON

THAT LOST FEELING

I see so many stuck clients! From clients who have everything in life and believe they should be 'happy' yet aren't, to clients that feel so trapped by their current life their bodies make them really sick. Lots of clients who hate their jobs, whose marriages are falling apart, teenagers who aren't coping with life, people who just can't seem to have anything go right for them and people who are just lost and not even sure what they are looking for.

Why do we get lost or stuck?

Men in particular get stuck because they acknowledge they now have 'responsibilities'. "How can I be who my soul wants me to be when I have a wife, three kids and a huge mortgage?" I have to take the kids to sport, my boss wants me to work overtime, I have to have the garden planted, I need to repair the fence, I need to help my neighbour, I have to help a friend out, I need to visit my parents.

Women might say, "I have a house to run, cook, clean, garden, wash, iron, fold clothes, and a husband to keep happy and kids who play sport, and doctors visits, a sick mum and I have to work to bring in more money."

Children and teenagers might say, "I have school and then swimming, I have to help with the chores, I need to do homework and practise my instrument."

Grandparents might say, "I have to babysit one day a week, still cook, clean, visit sick friends, help out in the community group and volunteer."

Everyone has their own list.

We get lost, we become overwhelmed, and feel so alone. We especially feel taken for granted, we feel exhausted, we feel no one cares. Our life becomes so busy and we can't stop. We don't listen to anyone else and especially not to ourselves. We try to do things for everyone to keep everyone else happy, yet why do we feel so miserable? We have no peace. We can even wonder, "What is the point?"

Our training for feeling lost and stuck starts at a very young age. We learn continuously how to block ourselves from listening to our soul.

Why?

Because we focus on everyone else! We stop listening to our bodies.

We become who everyone else wants us to be. We try to please everyone else and we stop listening to our souls.

We get sick and we take tablets. We hurt ourselves and we don't listen to our bodies, we can turn to drinking, smoking and taking drugs. We avoid things, we eat badly, we escape with TV, books and computer games. We become so busy that finding any time for ourselves seems impossible.

We have tried to become the person our mother wants, our father wants, our teacher wants, our spouse, our children, our siblings, our grandparents, our boss, our friends and anyone and everyone else!

What happens when we are little is that we find everything

works when we please the other people in our lives – we respond to praise – we are allowed to love ourselves today because mum loves me, or dad loves me and so it continues until there are so many people in our life that we are trying to keep happy that it becomes impossible. In trying to keep one person happy we disappoint the other person. The older we get, the more people we have in our lives and the more people we try to keep happy, the harder it gets!

I use this story often with young teenagers. Like all my stories though it is relevant to all ages.

BALLOONS
Imagine every single person in your life is a balloon. Take the first balloon – this can represent one of your parents perhaps. Now the aim of this game is to keep the balloon in the air by tapping it and not letting it hit the ground. This means you will always keep that balloon (person) happy! It's pretty easy with one balloon isn't it? Now add another balloon. It's still possible to keep both balloons up. Now add more balloons, each representing someone else you are trying to keep happy – teachers, friends, siblings, grandparents, bosses, work colleagues. Not only is it impossible to keep all these balloons in the air but I imagine you are now exhausted. This picture represents how most of us live our lives!

The only time we now feel peace is the one or two weeks a year when we go on holidays and no one bothers us! (There are no balloons to keep in the air!) It seems that on holidays everyone steps back and allows you space and you allow space for yourself, so you get peace. Thus begins the nightmare of nearly killing yourself trying to please everyone for a year just so that you get two weeks off to find your peace.

So what is a holiday? Most people will say: A holiday is time away from responsibilities, work, school, commitments, a time away from fulfilling everyone else's needs.

A holiday really is a feeling! It's a time where we give ourselves permission to relax, not to be overwhelmed by the pressures of life, to spend time with each other, to do things we enjoy.

My question to you is, why do we wait? Why wait to experience this once a year? The secret is to work out what things in your life give you this 'holiday feeling' and add them into your life EVERY DAY!

Here are some ideas you can try that clients and I have come up with during our sessions. The important thing with each of these ideas is that **while you are experiencing them, you acknowledge to yourself the feeling you get** – it just helps us to lock in the holiday feeling.

- Need to take the kids to after-school sport – play your favourite CD in the car.
- Doing housework – play music, sing, dance.
- The most important – turn off your TV! TV doesn't give you that holiday feeling it just helps you avoid your life and focus on other people's lives through TV series. When on real holidays most of us don't even think of watching TV!
- Light a fire mid-week and sit out under the stars, even if it is only for 10 minutes!
- Take a cup of tea or coffee outside and have it in the sun or under the stars.

- Run yourself a bath.
- Drive home in your slippers
- Make yourself a hot pack.
- Put a card game like Uno on your table (it's amazing how people will talk and laugh over cards).
- Change something for yourself. Be aware of how many balloons you are trying to keep in the air, because the more balloons we have on the go the more exhausted we will be. Begin to understand yourself and how and why you got here. Be gentle with yourself in the process.

This book isn't meant to make you give up your job and go save baby rhinos in Africa! It's meant to make you aware; to learn how to listen to yourself so you can work out how to love yourself. It's meant to make you bloom where you are planted! Not to want to run away from your life but to embrace it.

Your soul has got you here so far. It has never left, it is forever.

Here is exactly where you are meant to be right now! From now on, things will get easier because of the ability to hear what your soul is saying, the ability to focus on your soul emotions, which give you peace, joy and the ability to love yourself.

Everything changes when you start to emit your own frequency rather than absorbing the frequencies around you, when you start imprinting your intent on the universe rather than receiving an imprint from existence.

BARBRA MARCINIAK

LADDERS

LOST BY COMPARISON

Not only do we feel lost because we try to be who we think others want us to be, we also lose ourselves because we forget that our soul is unique, that being ourself, our soul self, is exactly who we are meant to be. Earlier we discussed our ability to love ourselves completely, absolutely 100% if we were the only one on our deserted island. So what happens to us when we add other people into that space?

We compete and we lose the ability to feel good about ourselves. Unknowingly, we compare ourselves to other people every minute of the day, trying to establish if we fit in, and if so, where we fit in. We respond only to Earth rules of what is okay, and how we should be, look and feel, and if we think people like us.

Unconsciously we refer to the Earth rule list:
- what our marks are at school?
- what job we do?
- how big our house is?
- what car do we drive?
- do our children achieve?
- how we dress?
- what we look like?

- how good we are at sport?
- what we eat?
- what we read?
- how we achieve?
- where we live?
- what we earn?
- how many Facebook friends we have?
- how many likes we get on a social media status?

The list is endless. I am sure you can all add in your own comparisons that you continually use. Our ability to love ourselves is based on, 'if we think others can and will love us'. Therefore we stop listening to who we are, to our soul, to us being okay and to having peace within ourselves, and we start comparing and competing with other people all day every day.

Comparison is the death of joy.

Mark Twain

Unknowingly we live by a life of ladders. We compare everything. By comparing ourselves we unconsciously start a ladder. We continuously compare ourselves to others to see where we fit in, or in ladder terms, what rung we place ourselves on. The lower down we are, the less ability we have to like ourselves, and the less we think others like us. We live our life looking at this ladder every day and referring to it in every single thing we do and every single thought we have.

Every single person in your life works with ladders. Parents, grandparents, children, bosses, teachers, schools, universities, governments, world organisations. Everyone you can think of refers to a ladder. So why don't ladders work for our soul selves. Ladders suggest that the person on the top of the ladder is superior to the people below them. This form of heriachy that our Earth self gets caught up in as a way to feel good about ourselves completely omits the fact that – We are all the same. We are souls having an Earth experience to try and work ourselves out. Our journey is ours, it's not better or worse than anyone else's no matter what we do, it's just ours. However, if we work on a heirachy system to immerse ourselves in Earth emotions then we stop the opportunity of listening, learning from, teaching to, communicating with and inspiring and being inspired with souls that can help us.

From sports stars, world leaders, famous singers to a mother, father, student, to an orphan in a third world country, we are all the same, we are all souls here trying to work ourselves out.

Let's look at how we can deal with ladders

- Jane's house is always clean.
- Jim spends time with his kids.
- Anna bakes.
- Jo's garden is beautiful.
- Matt gets A-plus in maths.
- Kym sings better.
- Alan kicks further.
- Richard's wife left him.

And so the list goes on.

TURN YOUR LADDER SIDEWAYS. Imagine if we could turn that ladder sideways. Imagine if we could see it from a soul's perspective.

- Jane, whose house is always clean – Jane's lesson is self-esteem.
- Jim who spends time with his kids – Jim's lesson is to feel connected.
- Anna who bakes – Anna's lesson is to feel nurtured.
- Jo the gardener – Jo's lesson is to learn to find peace.
- Matt who is a maths whiz – Matt's lesson is to find independence.
- Kym who can sing – Kym's lesson is trust.
- Alan who can kick a football – Alan's lesson is to believe in himself.
- Richard whose wife left him – Richard's lesson is to speak for himself.

Imagine if we could see this, and understand that every soul has its own plan to learn what they came here to learn. Then, maybe, we could find peace right here, right now, and embrace and love ourselves just for being our self. Maybe then we could hear just what our soul is trying to tell us.

PERSONAL EXAMPLE

Early on when I was still seeing clients at home, an appointment was made for a very successful businessman. I had worked in corporate a few years before and I was horrified that I was working in my bedroom. What was this man going to think of me? I had put myself on the bottom of the ladder! After discussions with my husband, he said,

"Babe, if you build it they will come!" He made me realise that if he comes to me then I am meant to help him, not judge him!

I turned my ladder sideways.

The man came and as we worked and talked, he cried for one-and-a-half hours. He had also put himself on the bottom of his ladder in relation to everyone else in his life! If we keep our ladders upright we can never help anyone. We are all equal no matter what we have or what we do. We are all just souls in Earth bodies learning to love ourselves.

When we have our ladder sideways, when we use comparisons to inspire us instead of destroying ourselves, then it is so much easier to love ourselves when we step back and look at a bigger picture. When we realise that words can often be the other person "trying to make us feel …", they use these words to help them feel good about themselves. They use these words to ladder climb. Every minute of the day we should make sure our ladder is sideways so that we can try to hear what a person's lessons are, not what their words are saying. Then we can try to understand why we react to their words in a certain way and what our lesson may be from this, and we can love them and ourselves better.

All of us are equal, all of us struggle, all of us need to turn our ladder sideways.

We will go into this a bit further later, but we need to understand ourselves better first.

I allow myself to be my own being.

DON VINEY

UNDERSTAND OUR EARTH TYPE

SAFE OR FREE

From our Earth experiences two types of people will be created:

One is a person who needs to feel safe. They tend to stay in the same job, same house, same marriage, they will be resistant to change, they will love snuggling up under a doona with a DVD. They move out later in life. They can often prefer to be at home instead of going out. Their safe-place feeling is in a tree, or a room, or a forest – somewhere that they can feel protected.

A person who needs to feel safe needs security. Risks are hard for them when they don't know what the outcome could be. They tend to let opportunities pass them by and stay stuck in the same situations, i.e. job, relationship, living space. They have lots of ideas about what they want in life but they can block themselves from achieving any of this.

The other is a person who needs to feel free. They love being on swings, they can feel trapped in relationships. They change jobs, they work in a free job – that is a job that doesn't lock them away, maybe a trade or working in and out of the office, like a salesperson or consultant. They move homes frequently, they travel, they have no fear of travelling by themselves, they run away from 'things'. They love the beach. They will have lots of different groups of friends. Their safe place will be a beach, or a meadow – somewhere where they feel like they can breathe, somewhere not confined.

A person who needs to be free always needs an out. If they are stuck in a house they need the curtains open, need to see a door! For a person who needs to feel free it's hard for them to commit to things.

All of us have both tendencies depending on the situation in front of us, but one feeling, either safe or free, will be dominant in your life. One feeling will influence all of the decisions you make without you being aware of that influence. Your soul doesn't have safe or free – we don't get this feeling genetically. This feeling will only come as a response to your personal Earth experiences and will stop you achieving what your soul wanted to achieve, leaving you feeling lost, disconnected and confused. The secret is not to hate or resent your safe or free, the secret is to embrace it, then you can understand yourself better. Then you are another step closer to connecting to your soul self and your path of what you wanted to achieve here.

SAFE AND FREE OR FREE AND SAFE

One will create the other. Safe will make free and free will make safe!

If you have a parent who needs to feel safe they will reflect that in every way. They will parent you based on what they need; they will help you with everything; they will ensure you feel safe at all times. You will get *so* well looked after that you may feel trapped, which will create in you the need to be free.

If you have a parent who is not there, either from working or through death, divorce or illness, or if you have a home which is unstable or even abusive through any of these reasons, then you might feel vulnerable, insecure, scared, and lose trust. Then you may become a person who needs to feel safe!

Interestingly, the youngest child of a large family, especially if there is a significant age gap, has so many parent figures in their childhood (siblings also telling them what to do) that ensures the youngest child feels 'safe' can often result with the youngest child in the family needing to feel free!

Safe and Safe – that is, you may be safe and your partner may be safe. This works because you will both be trying to create an environment that feels safe, so it is easier to relate to the other person's ideas and feelings about things. You must be careful, however, to recognise your combined need for safe otherwise you might not only block yourself but block each other. You may never take risks with anything because of the need for you both to feel safe. Your life can become quiet stagnant and you may feel like you never achieve anything, or that your life is passing you by and you can't make any decisions. Safe parents also risk their kids feeling so safe that they end up feeling trapped and thus need to feel free. This makes it much harder to parent them because you are now dealing with a safe and a free in a relationship. And unless we know and understand how safe and free works it can lead to a very volatile house, especially in teenage years.

Free and Free – these people often find each other on a holiday overseas. Life when you put a free and free together can be very adventurous and very easy. When partnered with the same base of free it is very easy to relate to the other person's feelings and ideas about things. Again you must be careful to recognise your combined need for free because you may have no boundaries! Drugs can be an issue because you are trying to keep the free feeling going. Together it may be difficult to grow roots and settle down anywhere; or even have secure jobs; or you may struggle to communicate because you both work shift work. Because of your desire to keep moving, free parents have jobs that require a lot of moving, and parent with lots of activity and freedom. This can lead to children that need to feel safe. Again, parenting the opposite can lead to a volatile house!

TO FIND WHICH TYPE OF PERSON YOU ARE

You probably already have an idea after reading through the safe and free descriptions. You can have feelings for both but either safe or free will influence you unknowingly in decisions you make in your life.

Ask yourself these five questions and your answers will help confirm which type of person you are. Pick both your best memory and your worst memory for each, then work out the feeling that you have from this memory. One will fall under safe and the other will fall under free.

1. What is my earliest memory?
   Best Memory   Feeling   Safe/Free
   Worst Memory   Feeling   Safe/Free

   (This is between 0–2. It doesn't need to be a conscious memory, this may

be a feeling instead: being wrapped in a blanket, or cuddled or in a bath or sleeping or crying.)

2. What memory do I hold between 2–6?
   Best Memory   Feeling   Safe/Free
   Worst Memory   Feeling   Safe/Free

   (Could be parents fighting, playing outside, home-cooked dinners, looking after siblings, holidays – if it's a holiday be careful to identify the feeling you had not the holiday itself!)

3. What memory do I hold between 6–11?
   Best Memory   Feeling   Safe/Free
   Worst Memory   Feeling   Safe/Free

   (Could be school memories, early friends, home environment.)

4. What memory do I hold between 12–18?
   Best Memory   Feeling   Safe/Free
   Worst Memory   Feeling   Safe/Free

   (Teenage years, friends, parents, high school, family, teachers.)

5. What memory do I hold between 19–25?
   Best Memory   Feeling   Safe/Free
   Worst Memory   Feeling   Safe/Free

   (First years as an adult, life after school, working, studying, socialising.)

Work out if your answers are feeling trapped, free, insecure or safe. You will have traits in both but one will be dominant.

Once you have worked out which one you are, you will see the pattern in your life and see how this base of safe or free may have influenced decisions in your life so far. Neither safe nor free is bad, it is just a fact. Once we recognise this we can begin to understand ourselves; why we have made certain choices in our life so far and why we block ourselves. We can now use this information to help us with every decision we make for the rest of our lives.

If you are a person that needs to feel safe, embrace your feeling of needing to be safe and add it to your life. Add things to your day that keep you feeling safe. It's not good or bad it is just a fact, a part of your response to your upbringing.

When you make life decisions, such as buying a house, starting a new job, what course to do, starting a business, travelling, where to live, but you feel blocked or never seem to be able to achieve it, work out, "OK, if I do this how can I help myself to still feel safe?" and then incorporate this into your new venture. Say you want to travel, then travel with someone else. If you want to do a course that relates to your job or the new job that you want, make sure you have access to advisors, or speak to people who have done it before. This will ensure you feel safe and at the same time unblock your path.

Or if you are a person that needs to feel free, once you recognise your need to feel free, go about ways of including free! For example, if you have a great job offer but you feel 'that trapped feeling' with it, work it out. Take a week off every three months (see, now you can breathe!). If you are married, plan a weekend away every now and again, work in the garden.

Embrace your feeling of being free and add it to your life. Add things to your day that keep you feeling free – even if it's a picture of a tropical island above your workspace!

When you make life decisions, such as buying a house, starting a new job, buying a shop, travelling, but you feel blocked, or never seem to be able to achieve it, work out, "OK, if I do this how can I help myself to still feel free?" Then incorporate this into you new venture.

Understand that the advice we give to others will be based on our safe or free status.

If we are dealing with someone who is struggling – what we think they need will actually be about us. That is, if you are a person who needs to feel safe, your advice will be based on what will make it better for you. That works if safe is dealing with safe and free is dealing with free. However, if you are dealing with the opposite it becomes much harder to understand them. Say your partner keeps leaving a conversation, or is having a moment when you don't want to go out, or is vomiting when you say you are pregnant, or your child won't come out of their room, or your girlfriend won't come over, etc., work out which type of person they really are, safe or free, and look at it and understand it from their base of safe or free. It helps so much with communication and understanding.

You see, we can take everything personally. Without first stopping to understand the situation, we assume the other person feels and responds to things the same way we do. Example: he never comes to my house (he's probably a safe and it's not really about you it's about him); she never texts me or calls me during the week (she is probably a free and thinks if it was her, she would hate someone smothering her so she gives space), this may be interpreted by a safe person as if she doesn't care.

It has been really interesting with many clients who have had ongoing issues with either or both parents, for many years and often say they feel like the black sheep in the family. For these clients, it's like an epiphany when they realise all the advice they have been given was for a safe person while they are actually a free person. They have spent their whole lives thinking something was wrong with them because following their advice just didn't feel right.

To help you be the person you are meant to be, you need to always look back to what type of person you are before you make any big decisions and incorporate how you can help yourself feel safe or free. This will help to prevent you blocking yourself, your path, or anyone else's.

I met a mum years ago who had embraced her need for free. Every night when her husband got home she would grab a wine or cup of tea and go into their home office to read the paper. It allowed her space so she wouldn't feel trapped.

If you are a woman that needs to be free, imagine how 'staying home' to raise the children would feel for you? If you are a woman that needs to feel safe, then you need to make your children safe. Imagine how going to work would feel for you.

If you are a man who needs to feel free imagine how the idea of an office job and huge family mortgage may feel for you.

If you are the parent of a free child who decides they want to go overseas for a year by themselves and travel aimlessly – with no job, no home base and no accommodation booked – imagine the kind of advice the safe parent would give to them.

Change your thoughts and you change your world.

NORMAN VINCENT PEALE

What you are allowed to see

Reality

Part 3
UNDERSTANDING OUR SOUL LESSONS ON EARTH

Someday everything will all make perfect sense. So for now, laugh at the confusion, smile through the tears, and keep reminding yourself that everything happens for a reason.

UNKNOWN

INTRODUCTION TO SOUL LESSONS

It may or may not surprise you but we do not come here to be an elite sports person, or a farmer, or a successful businessperson. We do, however, come here to learn and to learn we need to understand how we feel. That doesn't mean you shouldn't follow your dreams, or that you shouldn't have goals for what you want to achieve in life. It does mean that you need to understand yourself as you follow your dreams, because often when you get 'there' it may not be where you wanted to be! It just may not feel enough, and you won't have peace. Many famous people, singers, actors and elite sports people can suffer from depression, alcoholism and drug habits.

I spoke to a self-made multi-millionaire recently and he said something was missing even though he was told continuously he was 'successful'. Clearly what our Earth selves imagine to be successful, he was, and from an Earth perspective he should have himself on the top of the ladder. Yet no matter what he achieved he just didn't feel successful.

Many, many people I see say to me, I should be happy, I have everything a person could want – nice house, car, beautiful kids, great job, happy marriage – yet I feel so bad all the time. I just can't be happy, something must be wrong with me. The problem is they just haven't understood or embraced what their soul is trying to learn yet.

No matter what you do – an elite athlete, a single parent, a mother, a father, a farmer, a cleaner, a business owner, a famous singer, a student, a drug addict – or where you come from – a member of a royal family, a third world country, living in an upper class world, middle class world or living on the street – we are all the same, we are all here learning for our souls. We are all here to help each other. We all need to take time to understand what our lessons are. Even though our lives may be very different our lessons may not. The feelings that we have are an opportunity to understand ourselves and at the same time are often very similar feelings to how other people with completely different life experiences can feel.

Take a song that becomes an overnight hit. Why? Because so many people who instantly love it and buy it relate to the song. Why? Because each person's life experience, even though it may be different, gave them the same feeling. They relate to the song and the feeling that it gives them. We are not so different after all.

Instead of being grouped by colour – black people, white people, etc. – or by race – Australian, Indian, Sudanese, Asian, American, etc. – or by religion – Catholic, Protestant, Muslim, Jew, Buddhist, etc. – why can't we be grouped by soul lessons? Souls learning self-love, or souls learning empowerment, or souls learning understanding, or compassion, or acceptance, or to feel welcomed, or trust, hope, self-worth, or independence. That would make much more sense and it would make it much easier to help and understand each other.

The unexamined life is not worth living.

SOCRATES

Difficulties in your life don't come to destroy you, but to help you realise your hidden potential.

UNKNOWN

BEGINNING TO UNDERSTAND

It helps if we can put our Earth emotional responses aside for a moment and see it from a souls perspective.

So how do we understand our 'soul lessons'? Well let's go back to before you were born – because your soul was very much alive then.

Before any major project is undertaken we can assume that lots of planning and coordination goes into it. It is the same for our life on Earth. We come here only to learn more about our souls.

Say your soul is here to learn one or two of the following: peace, self-love, empowerment, understanding, compassion, acceptance, to be welcomed, trust, hope, self-worth, independence. In order for you to get the true opportunity to learn and really understand these states of being then you must really feel and live through the opposite state of that emotion.

It may be decided that you are to learn self-worth and independence, so before you are born a soul (maybe from your soul group) sits next to you and you compare lists of what you both want to learn on Earth, and the soul says: "I love you so much that I will come to Earth and ...

- I promise I will help to teach you self-worth;
- I won't give up until you have learnt it properly;
- I will leave you;
- I will take away your power;
- I will give you stressful experiences;
- I will provide an environment where you will continuously get the opportunity to learn through each other's actions exactly what it is you want for this life lesson," and you get to do the same for them. (Lessons are never one way.)

This happens many times with many different souls planning ways to help our souls learn what they really want to learn.

Then, you come to Earth and while a soul person (say a parent to start with) is trying to learn say self-esteem – because they suffer from depression, or OCD, or are very abusive etc., and at the same time you want to learn independence, inner strength, self-worth and empowerment, etc., so you become their child. You are now both soul teachers for each other.

Your childhood experiences helps give us the first insights into what your soul is trying to learn.

You may have lived with an OCD parent, bi-polar parent, depressed parent, an abusive parent, an over-protective parent, a controlling parent, a mentally ill parent, or you may have had lessons from other people, an uncle or aunt, brothers or sisters, school peers, teachers, family friends. Anyone who invokes a feeling in you is helping you to learn, they are giving you an opportunity to understand yourself. The following are general examples from working with clients. The emotions may or may not relate to your individual circumstances but it is to give you a general idea of how life experiences work.

Let's look at depression – say one of your parents had severe depression – what was in it for you? Well think about how you felt – inadequate, responsible, guilty, trapped.

Say someone in your family suffered from a mental illness. How did you feel – abandoned, overlooked, unimportant?

Say you were poor. How did you feel – like a victim, defeated, powerless, angry, deprived?

Say you were abused. How did you feel – scared, shattered, powerless, unloved, overlooked, worthless?

Say you were bullied. How did you feel – alone, unlovable, unwelcome, disconnected?

Both people in any situation are continuously given opportunities to learn what their soul wanted. Both of you will be teaching the other one. Both of you are soul teachers.

If we look over our childhood it's not the experience that is important, it's how you feel. From there we can embrace the feelings, instead of trying to avoid them in every area of our lives. By avoiding these feelings we just block ourselves in our life from the potential we have and who we are meant to be. We unconsciously block doing or having anything to do with things or people that make us feel the way we did in childhood. To embrace it means to understand it – it means to understand yourself.

PERSONAL EXAMPLE

When I was little I was the middle child, I felt at times unwelcome especially at school and that no one liked me and that I didn't fit in. As an unconscious response to this I friend-hopped. That is I had two or more groups of friends so I could just pop in to each group, unconsciously trying to feel welcome yet still always feeling unwelcome. I never really gave one group of friends the chance.

Now I am aware that this is something that I do – it is part of me, a tendency to feel unwelcome, so I embrace it. If I am with a group of friends and I feel the familiar feeling of unwelcome I can smile at myself, take a deep breath and know it's just me – my perception of things – and I don't need to find things in the conversation or people's actions to help me feel unwelcome, I can just let the feeling pass and enjoy the company I am with.

People come into your life at different times for different reasons. Sometimes they stay a while, sometimes they are just passing through, but all of these people come for a reason. They give us an opportunity to learn something new about ourselves and we will do the same for them.

We meet no ordinary people in our lives. If you give them a chance everyone has something amazing to offer.

UNKNOWN

In order to move on, you must understand why you felt what you did and why you no longer need to feel it.

MITCH ALBOM

UNDERSTANDING AND EMBRACING LESSONS

Why do tragic things happen, why do we get abused, hurt, why do we go through horrible experiences?

From an Earth perspective – which includes all the Earth emotions like justice, fear, hurt, pain, destruction, humiliation, right and wrong, anger, disempowerment, abandonment, unloved, revenge, overwhelmed, exhaustion, horror and despair, emotional trauma, etc., I am with you. There have been times in my life where I can't rationalise people's behaviour, and as an Earth person will never understand why people have to experience such traumatic experiences. However, if I really tune into my soul, I can see the why – I can see what that person is trying to experience and I can see from the emotion they feel what they are trying to learn. I can see what their soul teacher is trying to achieve.

PERSONAL EXAMPLE

For as long as I can remember I had an issue with trust. Trusting people, trusting the universe, trusting that things would work out, trusting life. I was a control freak because that helped me deal with my lack of trust in things. Being a control freak helped me to feel like I could control life.

My daughter Danielle died when she was four-and-a-half – she had an asphyxiating asthma attack. In the lead up to her death she hadn't been sick, in fact quite the opposite. She had had her nanna sleep over with her, she had written letters to her two best friends and posted them the day before, she had written Nick's name (her little brother) on her Buzz Lightyear toy, she had put her favourite doll in Steph's cot (her little sister) and she slept in our bed the night before she died.

So when she died my world was shattered and whatever trust I had in anything was shattered along with it. As the months went by and I looked back, part of me wondered whether she knew. I believe she did – not consciously but somehow part of her knew and she was doing what she could to help.

Then 10 months later I found out I was pregnant. I was so scared and again any trust in life that I had regained completely disappeared. Now some 14 years later I can see the positive in this from a soul perspective (my Earth mother side still pops her head up questioning). But from a soul perspective I was trying to learn trust – the opposite to how I felt – to trust there is a plan, there is a purpose, to trust in life, the universe, to TRUST unconditionally, TRUST. And truly trusting gives you PEACE which makes Earth feel like heaven!

I read a book a few years ago, *The Five People You Meet In Heaven* by Mitch Albom. This book for me was like a light bulb turning on, just like when you get something!

Eddie had died and was meeting five different people in heaven. When I started reading this book I assumed when you go to heaven you meet the people you love, have the hug, etc.

Eddie's father had what we would say on Earth, 'mistreated' Eddie – through neglect, violence and silence. Eddie held onto a lot of hate and anger to do with his dad and the way he was brought up, blaming his dad for why he had failed at times to achieve what he thought he should have.

The people Eddie meets in this book were a complete surprise to him, however the impact they had on each other's lives to ensure he was on the right path was undeniable.

The books aim is to help us to be aware that good and bad people will be in our life for a reason. You may not have known the reason at the time, but that is what you will discover in the first stage of heaven.

CLIENT EXAMPLE

Gabrielle, 30 years old – when she was 20 she caused a car accident that resulted in the death of another young woman. The young woman that died left behind a husband and a child. Gabrielle has always looked at this from Earth emotions and struggled to love herself or forgive herself which in kinesiology terms is what we call a block. She is unable to move forward in her life, she is stuck in Earth rules – what she thinks everyone else will think – guilt, blame, fear of success, unworthiness.

Soul perspective – these two had met before they both came here. Both these souls were trying to achieve something. She helped a soul move on which was always the plan – her goal was to learn to love herself BIG TIME – perfect as souls, they are like best friends, they may even be part of the same soul group. Both there to love and support each other.

As a human, Gabrielle thought she needed to destroy herself – blaming herself especially when years later she gave birth to her own child. She was not free to love or find her peace. We did a huge balance in removing her from being 'stuck' in time and clearing her to love herself – when discussing this whole situation from a soul perspective for the first time it became clear it was like she remembered she had made this plan and it was actually a privilege to fulfil her role in this pact. Now she would have an opportunity to put all her effort into learning to love herself. In the place before here (heaven or pre-Earth place) we can't identify with Earth emotions so we forget how intense they can be, especially when we live in a world of what other people think. Also our Earth time is such a short time that we don't, as soul people before, appreciate the intensity and how two years of Earth time can actually feel like a really long time. It can feel like an even longer time when we look at it and live in Earth emotions.

The beauty of Gabrielle now seeing this from a soul perspective is she realised that she had a very special friend in heaven, someone that loved her unconditionally. She could now look to her as her soul person, that she could pray to, ask for guidance. She could choose to finally be free to love herself.

To understand yourself and your past:
You need to push all your feelings
to the sides then reach in and pull out
the emotion that you felt. Look at that
emotion and flip it. The positive word
for that emotion is exactly what you and
your soul is trying to learn.

MEL RYAN

Self-Worth: Sometimes your greatest teachers in life had no idea just what they taught you. Especially those who treated you the worst. The day you said, "I deserve much better than this," was the day you graduated from their class.

UNKNOWN

FORGIVENESS

Forgiveness doesn't mean that we say what you did is okay. Forgiveness just means we have found peace in the situation. Forgiveness means we understand ourselves, we understand what we were trying to learn.

Forgiveness does not mean that everything is okay. Forgiveness means that you realise that a person is limited in their ability to love you how your Earth person wants to be loved. It means your Earth person may never understand their actions but your soul person can see a bigger picture. It means that the person who taught you by hurting you can now be let go, their choice of actions can no longer inhibit your life. It also means that you can see them as a soul teacher and not an Earth person. You see the bigger picture, you embrace that picture and yourself and you understand the lesson in it for you, or what I like to say, you get the 'why'.

Our souls attract people, experiences and situations into our lives to help us learn. The people who give us the hardest times are often the souls that love us the most. I know from an Earth perspective that it's hard to believe, but when we really think about it, the people that give us the hardest times are the ones that teach us the most or at least give us the biggest opportunity to learn – soul teachers.

It is a really hard concept to get your head around, especially when abuse is involved. And by no means is this statement making light of a traumatic situation. However, if we can let go of Earth emotions for a second and look at things from a soul perspective, it can give us a whole new insight into life. If we let go for a second of focusing on what was done to us and focus instead on understanding our feeling or feelings, then in turn we can look at what we are/were trying to learn.

A DIFFERENT VIEW

I walked past an angel calendar one day and the thought for the day was up, it read, "Your parents love (or loved) you to the best of their ability." I stopped and thought about this. To me this meant that, yes, they might love you to the best of their ability and give all they are able to give no matter how limited and this is okay. However it is also okay if, for you, this wasn't good enough or it wasn't what you felt you needed.

It means that you can acknowledge both sides of this situation. That it wasn't good enough – that is okay, and that they gave all they could give – that is also okay. It's just a fact. It takes the anger and the blame away in it not being okay. It allows you not to have guilt. It allows you to forgive them, or rather find your peace in this situation, and at the same time you don't have to pretend nothing happened to you. They just couldn't do any better than they did. This is the same for every situation and life experience.

Imagine you have an egg carton with 12 spaces for eggs or in other words you need 12 eggs to help you feel loved. If your parent only has 2 eggs to give you, then they will give you everything they possibly can and still be 10 eggs short. The beauty of this situation is that there is 10 egg spaces free in which we need to be responsible to allow that to be filled. There will be so many times in our life when others, situations and ourselves has and will have the opportunity to fill the gaps in our egg carton. The problem is that we can become focused on how unfair it is that our parents don't fill our egg carton. If we deal with the fact they only ever had a 2 egg giving capacity, and giving us everything they can they were only ever going to fill 2 egg spaces. If we deal with facts then we can be grateful and even appreciative of what our parents gave us and find peace in that. We can then look forward to all the interesting and amazing ways that we now get to fill our egg carton.

FREE YOURSELF – UNDERSTAND THE SOUL NOT THE ACTIONS

It's very hard to understand people's actions when you're dealing with situations like rape, abuse, people cheating on you, etc., so how do we look at this?

Even though we hate that person's Earth actions, that person has given us a learning opportunity. Sometimes it may be the biggest of our lives. So, instead of focusing on them and what they did, (let's take them totally out of the picture) let's focus on our self. What could possibly be our lessons in this?

- Did we lose our self-esteem?
- Did we become scared of life?
- Did we feel lost and abandoned?
- Did we have to become independent at a very early age?

- Did we feel unloved and unwelcomed?
- Did we lose trust in life?

All of these are major life lessons and we can do one of two things. We can stay there stuck, feeling like a victim, like everything bad happens to us, we can have no power, we can blame everything else and continue to rely, albeit limitedly, on other people for help.

We can begin to embrace our lessons, to look, not at what happened (I think if it's that traumatic the first time why relive it?) but at what learning opportunities we got from it. Begin to understand the feelings that this situation brought up for you and work out what the opposite is to that.

For example, you lost all trust. In that case, we work on how you can get trust back into your life – not from anyone giving it to you but by working out how *you* can bring trust back into your life.

If it's self-esteem, look at your ability to empower yourself and ways you can help yourself.

If it is rejection or abandonment then understand this about yourself. Embrace that it is part of you and look at ways to help yourself feel included and accepted. Don't rely on other people's actions to help you feel included and accepted – it's your job to find how you can do it.

Every experience, no matter how traumatic or joyful, has a hidden message inside it that is just for us. It's like a secret present in life. An experience with messages in it for us to help understand our souls and what we are learning. It's kind of like eating a chocolate filled with caramel – we need to bite right into the middle to find the good bit!

Often when we are older, when souls have really learnt what it is they wanted, their relationships with their 'soul teachers' will completely change. If your dad or mum, really your 'soul teacher', works out that you understand, that you have learnt what your goal was to learn – you believe in yourself the way your soul wants – then all of a sudden things change, you get along, you really enjoy each other's company, you say yes, he or she's changed so much. That is because you embraced what it is you were meant to learn so he or she didn't need to teach you anymore. I have seen many clients' relationships change for the better with their parent or parents, spouses and children, etc., as my clients' ability to understand and embrace the experience frees them both from the teaching and learning cycle.

CLIENT EXAMPLE

A beautiful example of this is one of my clients, Rose, 26 years old. She was suffering from anxiety and panic attacks. She had grown up in a very controlled, violent and abusive house, very powerless, often beaten to unconsciousness by her father. Her mother, aware of the violence, was too scared to stand up to her husband. She had not spoken to her parents for 12 months. The combination of guilt she had from not talking to them and fear, rejection, hurt, disbelief, anger and feeling powerless had certainly not left her even though she no longer saw her parents.

We worked together over a few months. Going through not so much what happened but how she felt, what she was trying to learn, what everyone's roles were. Essentially helping her work through her life from a soul perspective.

She has since not only reconciled with her parents but they came to the end of their soul teaching learning cycle.

You see she didn't go back to them to say sorry and continue on as if nothing happened. If she had done this the same or similar thing would have happened with the same feelings involved because their souls were still trying to teach each other lessons.

Instead she went back – she bit the chocolate right into the middle and said why? She listened, she talked. She embraced exactly what her soul was meant to learn, what their souls were trying to teach her and it gave her parents the opportunity to do the same. Her parents also embraced the opportunity. She looked at it from a soul perspective and taught them to do the same. Over a few months of real talking their relationship changed. Now they have a very loving and peace-filled relationship.

It doesn't always work out like this. However, our job as souls is to learn and to give others the opportunity to learn. Sometimes when we give others the opportunity to learn they don't react well, we need to learn to have peace within ourselves and remind us we gave them an opportunity to learn, to change and to invite peace into their lives. It is not our responsibility if they don't take it.

CLIENT EXAMPLE

I had a client text me the other day saying, "Mel you would be so proud of me. I woke up with a sore throat and a cough and thought to myself, hmmm what is this all about? I realised that I was very angry at my roommate and she is actually driving me nuts and really annoying me!" That's wonderful

I replied (knowing she hated and avoided confrontation). I asked her what she was going to do about it? "Why? Do I have to do something about it? I know what it is all about!" she replied.

"You should be proud of you for that," I said. "However, if your body has manifested this then your soul is asking you to deal with it not just acknowledge it. I understand your fear in talking to her about it because you don't want to hurt her feelings and you are scared how she might react. However, unless she is aware by someone telling her that what she does is annoying then she can never change. Think of it as if you are giving her a present – you are giving her a learning opportunity!"

"WOW that's awesome," she replied. "Thanks."

The mind is everything.

What you think you become.

BUDDHA

THEMES

Most people will be able to find a theme in their life – the older you are the easier it is. Through working with people I have found that as we look back over people's lives they will have a similar feeling going on in all of their major experiences. They go through a situation, which may be similar to someone else's, but the feeling they take from that experience will be the one that is relevant to them.

It's like two people walking through a meadow, Sarah and Michelle. Sarah is attracted to blue flowers so as she walks through the meadow she picks all the blue flowers. Michelle, however, is attracted to yellow flowers so as she walks through the meadow she picks all the yellow flowers.

It's the same with emotions. Sarah and Michelle have the exact same experience, they both walk into a room and have to sit at a table where they don't know anyone. As they are seated, two other girls at the table whisper together. Instantly Sarah feels rejected (something she doesn't realise is her theme feeling, rejection is like finding blue flowers – she finds the opportunity to feel rejected in every situation she can). Her soul is trying to learn the opposite of rejection, to truly feel accepted and loved. This is something she has to do, no one can give it to her.

However, having the exact same experience walking into the room, Michelle instantly feels inadequate (something she doesn't realise is her theme feeling, inadequate is like her finding yellow flowers – she finds the opportunity to feel inadequate in every situation she can). Her soul is trying to learn to feel the opposite of inadequate, empowered and confident. In actual fact, the two girls at the table may have been talking about the time or something equally as irrelevant. Sarah and Michelle will always interpret a situation using issues related to them and what their soul is working on.

When I help people look back over their life we can see patterns of feelings. These are feelings that have been repeated since childhood, teenage years, young adulthood, parenting, middle age, retirement and senior years. When we do this they then work out with amazement that, yes, I do this all the time. That even in the safest of situations, with their family or friends that they can still feel what their theme is, i.e. rejected, abandoned, worthless, etc., and that they avoid many things or situations they would have loved to be part of because they are trying to avoid the same feeling, which is their theme. In fact they have blocked many opportunities in their life because of this.

Some of the major themes we deal with are:
- Fear
- Rejection
- Abandonment
- Being overlooked
- Inadequacy
- Powerlessness

- Worthlessness/unworthiness
- Lack of trust
- Deprived
- Unloved/unlovable
- Self-esteem/self-respect/self-worth

If we look back on our lives and keep dealing with feeling rejected, then this is what to start looking at, and why that experience keeps being attracted into your life, or why that is the feeling you get from your life experiences. Once you work out what your theme is, it is easier to be able to keep your power and find positives in all kinds of circumstances.

If you go into a situation knowing you are likely to take a certain feeling from it, that now means because you are aware of it, you can put things in place to help you take a positive feeling from that situation. Now you have your power back by understanding yourself better. Now you can be your soul self.

I explain this to my clients as: "to embrace it, it's like you put space between it". Something happens and instantly an emotional feeling, an emotional response comes up. Before you act on this feeling you give it space. Space to think why does this get to me? space to understand why this gets to me? and when you process that, you can respond in an empowered way.

For example, if Sarah was aware her pattern was to feel rejected then she could embrace it. She instantly feels rejected so she adds space to it before she responds, she understands that rejection is her theme. She could smile at herself when her feeling of being rejected presented itself as she reacted to the girls talking and instead of withdrawing and using every moment of the night to confirm she was rejected she could remind herself that she accepts herself, she chooses to love who she is and it doesn't matter what others think. She can and will be herself. Then the two girls get to see the real Sarah who isn't withdrawing from life. It's the same with Michelle – if she was aware her pattern was to feel inadequate then she could embrace it. She could smile at herself when her feeling of inadequacy presented itself as she reacted to the girls talking and instead of withdrawing and using every moment of the night to confirm she was inadequate she could then remind herself that she empowers herself, she chooses to love who she is and it doesn't matter what others think. She can and will be herself. Then the two girls get to see the real Michelle. The beauty of this is that when we are our soul selves we give other people the opportunity to do the same thing.

Love yourself for all you have been,

all you are, and all you will become.

UNKNOWN

> The secret of change is to focus all of your energy, not on fighting the old, but on building the new.
>
> — SOCRATES

WORKING OURSELVES OUT

Whatever happens to us, how we respond will be different. How we instantly react with our emotional feeling or emotional response will always be about us and what we need to learn. Two similar experiences can happen but two people can respond completely differently. Two people may have the same physical problem, i.e. not being able to get pregnant, back pain, migraines, illness, etc. The reason behind pain, illness or not being able to get pregnant will be different for each person. It's custom-made so to speak!

CLIENT EXAMPLE

A client came to see me. Although she loved her husband she was struggling to have a sexual relationship with him – she was sexually abused from age 13 to 16 by her uncle. To this day her mother still sees that uncle. She has no power. So when someone makes advances towards her, i.e. her husband, she is still in 13-year-old time. She freezes and sex feels like someone is doing stuff to her – no power and no control. She has never experienced sex from feeling how her body feels, she has sex with her mind and thoughts present and all of her energy going to feeling out of control. She has never experienced how to just be in time and enjoy her body for how it feels. She never explored her body or found joy in sex unless influenced by alcohol. Sex is an issue of vulnerability and for her it continues to take away her personal power. She has no choice but to react this way, it's in her programming. She needs to understand this in herself. We work on clearing the belief systems that leave her no choice so she can feel peaceful pleasure and not vulnerability.

CLIENT EXAMPLE

A client came to see me who had been abused from age 8 to 15 by her uncle. Her mother still sees that uncle. She cannot get enough sex, but when she has sex she totally needs to dominate. They may make the first advance but she then totally takes over and controls the whole sex act. This is her, controlling aggressively and needing to dominate. This is because having control in sex makes her feel safe. She has no choice but to react this way, it's in her programming. She needs to understand this in herself. We work on clearing the belief systems that leave her no choice so she can feel peaceful pleasure and not aggression.

Sex and sexual relations is a topic that comes up a lot with clients. How we respond to things is directly related to the belief systems that we gather along the way. I see many clients, both men and women, who seek help in this area, who don't embrace sex as a wonderful part of their life. Before you have a sexual encounter you are taught all about it by your parents, grandparents, social media and churches. You are given a set of rules to live by. You already have an opinion. Perhaps along the lines of, don't touch your body that's wrong, sex is dirty, or sex is not something that you discuss with anyone.

CLIENT EXAMPLE

A client had broken up with her husband a few years earlier and had recently met a man. She wanted to continue her relationship with him but she was scared. She had never had an orgasm and had never really enjoyed sex, in fact sex to her felt like a chore. We discussed all her feelings about sex and her first sexual experience. She had been brought up with religious beliefs about sex. She had had sex with a boy that she liked but they were not married at the time. She had never explored her body by herself. I explained that every time she had sex, she had sex with her mind, her thoughts and the belief systems she had, and not her body. She had actually never felt sex properly.

We discussed how she thought 'God' had got everything else right, but with physical bodies it just didn't work! I explained to her that 'God' didn't get it wrong, we did. We are actually designed for two people to have sex and you are meant to orgasm at the same time not before, not after, we just keep having sex with our minds! We did some work around this and clearing her stuck belief systems and then we came up with a plan: she needed to practise how her body felt not her mind. To start with she could rub moisturiser in and feel how it feels for her body, she could get to know her own body. She needed to learn body-feeling sex with her head out of it. The ability to reach orgasm is quite simply letting go, and just being in that moment. I can report she is a very happy girl now and has a wonderful sex life.

You are a living magnet. What you attract into your life is in harmony with your dominant thoughts.

BRIAN TRACY

HINTS WE ARE GIVEN

If we can take away everyone else then we truly have the ability to love ourselves – our soul person. So how can we take away everyone else when we live on Earth?

Our soul won't give up. It can't. It is ours forever, so we need to learn to listen to it. To do that we need to understand what our bodies are telling us. Our bodies will always tell us what is going on, what our soul is trying to learn. That is the only reason we are here. However, we live with no regard to how amazing this is. Our bodies tell us everything about ourselves we have just never been taught to listen.

> The right side of our bodies means male, career.
> The left side means female and family.
> Blood is spiritual.
> Bones means structure on Earth.
> Digestive system means how we digest life.
> Lungs mean how we take life in.
> Back means our ability to support ourselves.
> Bowels mean how we let go of things.
> Kidneys and bladder mean how we process life.
> Shoulders mean responsibility.

Bodies continuously heal themselves. In fact all our bodies have dealt with and beaten cancer many times and we will be completely unaware of it. You can actually have tonsillitis without knowing. In fact your tonsils can be full of pus and you feel no pain. This is just the body's way of clearing bacteria.

Bodies are amazing and will always try to heal themselves, often without us knowing, so why does it go wrong?

Bodies will always tell us what is going on with us physically, mentally, spiritually and emotionally. It is the perfect way for our souls to communicate with us, especially when we haven't been listening. In fact, we have just never been taught and aren't aware that we should listen.

Organs in our bodies hold emotions. Sometimes understanding what these are can help us understand ourselves. The information here is just the basics. There is much research that has been done on this and there is much more in-depth information around.

Heart	Love and Self-Esteem
Small intestine	Internalisation and Sorrow
Stomach	Empathy and Sympathy
Spleen	Rejection and Faith in the future
Lung	Regret and Depression
Large intestine	Grief and Guilt
Kidney	Fear and Anxiety
Bladder	Inadequacy and Inner Direction
Liver	Anger and Resentment
Gall bladdeer	Helplessness and Self-righteousness

There are some wonderful books which you can consult if you want to understand this further. *You Can Heal Your Life* by Louise L. Hay, or *The Body Is The Barometer Of The Soul* by Annette Noontilare or *Metaphysical Anatomy* by Evette Rose, I often use these books to see which definition may fit the person I am working with, and sometimes I will look it up on the internet under 'Spiritual Meaning of…'

People often go to elaborate measures to hurt themselves, doing terrible injuries to themselves while doing the simplest things, like falling over at a party and breaking their ankle, or putting on their socks and their back goes, or tripping up a step and knocking themselves out! The truth is these injuries or illnesses have been lurking in the background for some time, we just haven't taken the hint, so now we get the full opportunity to embrace what our body is telling us. The more pain we have the more emotion is involved.

PAIN = AN EMOTION

You cannot have pain anywhere in your body without there being an emotion that goes with it. It's your soul's way of trying to get your attention.

It is in fact quite simple and quite literal. If your throat hurts, you could be holding on to something you want to say or have said something you regret and need to deal with.

So, if you hurt your right foot, your soul is telling you that you need to look at moving forward regarding something to do with a male or your career.

Right shoulder means you need to think about whether you are taking on too much responsibility for males in your life or your career.

Left hand means you are not handling well something to do with a female or your family.

Ribs are not feeling protected.

CLIENT EXAMPLE

One of my teenage clients came in and had hurt her ribs playing soccer. It was on her right side and she was in a lot of pain. In discussion I discovered that she has a boy at school that was almost stalking her and making her feel uncomfortable. He was always trying to sit next to her and hug her whenever he could. So by having sore ribs she actually prevented anyone from hugging her and she kept the pain because she couldn't resolve the situation. She didn't want to be unkind to him even though she was extremely uncomfortable in his presence. How amazingly clever is her body manifesting a way to protect itself.

We did some work and actually balanced her on her ability to stand in her power, to know what is right for her, and her ability to talk to him – to say what she needed to say without taking on responsibility for his feelings or his response (how he felt and how he responded was his issue to deal with). I saw her a week later. She had spoken with him and said how she felt – after all it was just a fact (a truth), she explained how uncomfortable she was and asked him to back off. She took no responsibility for his feelings, which ended up with him being quite understanding, to her surprise. She was back on the soccer field pain free. Her body had nothing left to tell her or for her to deal with so it healed itself. She also gave him an opportunity to learn. Instead of him continuing to hug all the girls to help him feel accepted he could look at other ways to do this. He could also see how they felt.

Say you severed your leg and you still found you got phantom pains – it's because you still need to deal with why this happened! You still need to understand what your body is trying to tell you.

If you have large intestine problems it may be to do with guilt or grief. If you have a bladder infection you are probably 'pissed off' at something or someone. Your body can tell you a lot about yourself and what is going on!

One of my husband's friends, Mark, came to a barbeque at our house. He came in limping. He explained that his leg was sore and that he kept getting abscesses on his right thigh. So I casually asked him what was going on at work, are you really angry there at the moment – he nearly fell off the chair. How do you know that he asked? I replied, oh your body is trying to tell you, right leg is male and career and pus and pain is anger that you haven't talked about. Have you also had a sore throat? Yes, he said, quite surprised. In fact he had been promised a promotion every month for the last five months but his boss kept making excuses saying he would look at it next month and that he was too busy. Instead of Mark talking to him properly, he just took his anger home with him (by the way his 'theme' emotion was overlooked! This had happened to him before which is why his body was manifesting this abscess so he could finally look at the situation).

If you have an earache, you don't want to hear something.

PERSONAL EXAMPLE

When my daughter was 12 months old she developed an ear infection. I was trying to work out why as my husband and I had not been in any conflict. Then I listened to my house! My other two older children were arguing over games, food, whose turn it was, etc. – not aggressively but loudly at times!

I gave my daughter a balance (a kinesiology session) and discovered she had a very, very low tolerance to conflict. When something affects you, you can't change the other people, you can only investigate, understand and clear why you react that way to something.

She is born under what some people call the 'Crystal Children' (*The Crystal Children* is a book by Doreen Virtue) and they are the peace-makers of this world – so conflict really affected her deeply. So that's what we cleared, her reaction to conflict between other people.

Her body was able to tell us what her soul needed and that's why she got an ear infection. Her soul was asking her to look at something, namely her reaction to conflict, as she needed to clear this. Had we not cleared this she would have suffered more and more ear infections when conflict arose and her soul was trying to tell her to look at it. What happens when we cannot understand or don't listen to our bodies is we then take pain killers and antibiotics and may have to have grommets or suffer burst eardrums. Our soul will always carry this issue of not being able to deal with conflict well, and every chance it gets it will tell us. As we get older it may change to sore throats, chest infections or laryngitis, not saying how we feel, not getting things off our chest and not being able to speak as our true self. The soul will never give up trying to tell us what we need to look at.

That is why, when two people are in the same accident one can walk away unscathed, a miracle they say, whilst the other can be badly hurt and require months of rehabilitation. The second person's soul has been asking and asking for them to look at what they came here to learn.

Sinus issues mean someone close to you is annoying you! (It may even be yourself!)

PERSONAL EXAMPLE

I received a phone call from one of my son's teachers, telling me he was behind in his work. About 10 minutes later I complained to Steph that my right sinus was sore. We both burst out laughing amazed at how quickly the body works! One could assume from this that if I grounded my son until his work was complete then my sinus would be fine. But that's our Earth way of thinking – we think we need to fix things. It wasn't so much that I had to deal with my son, it was my body's way of telling me I had an issue with this. My issue with this was actually two things: one, being annoyed, not at him but at myself, because I cannot make him do what I want him to do and what I think is best for him which leaves me feeling inadequate. I had to let go of this and remind myself to trust him, to trust that his soul will help him learn what he is meant to learn; and two, being unconsciously influenced by what others think. I want him to do well in school because in our Earth world if he does well in some ways it reflects onto me as a parent and then I can feel good about myself. Both of these feelings turned me into what I call an 'Earth Mum'.

LIFE CHANGING EVENTS

Big life-changing events like illness, accidents, etc., don't just randomly happen. Usually the person has been getting lots of signs which they have never listened to, or life-changing events happen to put us on the correct path.

Maybe if they do have a sore throat, they go to the doctor to get antibiotics. This might kill the bug but the soul is not done talking yet so it will send you the same thing or something else. It will get bigger and bigger until you listen!

Cancer is a major one – it's like a near death experience. You cannot get cancer that you are aware of without anger. It's holding on deeply to a hurt that you have experienced but not understood. Your body and your life experience, have given you many opportunities to understand and embrace it, however, you have blocked it – so your body goes to drastic measures to get your attention. Where it is in the body can help give you an idea of what it is about. Breast cancer is about nurturing, lung cancer is about taking in life, bowel cancer is about grief and/or guilt.

Many people change lots of things both physically and spiritually when going through cancer. That is why they heal – the soul realises, yes, they get it. Now they have time to continue on their journey on Earth with a new soul perspective.

However, some people get cancer and have it cut out without changing or looking at anything, only to find the cancer returns or appears somewhere else. You see the soul is determined, it will never give up on you. It will always tell you what is going on by using your body even though you may ignore it.

Many people have life altering accidents. Some lose an arm or a leg, some could be paralysed, some could lose their sight, or have a stroke that leaves them permanently disabled, some could be struck down with an illness that stops them from the life they used to have. Does this mean they were given chances and didn't listen? No, not always. Sometimes it means you are literally just changing paths. You spent the first years gaining skills and information in one area and now you get to put those skills and attributes to good use while you gather more. It's kind of like a bonus round, two life experiences in one. When I have worked with these clients in the past, what they struggle with the most is letting go of what they used to do. Instead of focusing on the 'I can't', we move their focus to what they can do and are meant to do now. That is, if it was playing golf then it's not actually golf that they miss, it's the feeling golf gave them. So we go through how they felt when they played golf. Then we look at this feeling and try to experiment with other things that give them the same feeling. It's their job to keep trying new things until they find something that fulfills them.

CLIENT EXAMPLE

I treated a 29-year-old man who was once very fit and active. He had been a builder and in his last job he had been promoted to foreman. He had prided himself on everyone being amazed at the work he did. He also felt good about himself because everyone was envious of how good his body looked. In fact his whole self-esteem and ability to like himself was wrapped up in what he did and not at all in who he was. He came to see me because he had had an accident.

He had fallen through the roof of a building he was working on and severed his spinal cord. He was paralysed from the waist down. He had no feeling and no function in his lower limbs. His only focus was on trying to regain full function to his legs. He was trying everything he could to recreate the person he was. His focus was not on who he really is. We had to focus on him looking forward not backwards, finding the 'I can'. Finding out that who he really was had actually never changed. And that he had never taken the time to get to know himself through his eyes before. His soul had literally stopped him in his tracks and put him on the path he needed to be on. It just took him a while to work that out.

AUTO IMMUNE SYSTEM ILLNESSES

Chronic Fatigue Syndrome, fibromyalgia, rheumatoid arthritis and many more auto immune illnesses are becoming more prevalent today especially in our youth and in what appears to be once very healthy people. Why? To recover from such a life changing illness you have to change your life. An illness like this makes you follow soul rules. You have to listen to your body to find what works for you on a daily basis. You have to change your expectations of not looking at where you fit on the ladder compared to everyone else, but to appreciate what you can do no matter how little some days. You need to look after your body with good nutrition, and you can't put any thought into what others think because with an illness that you can't see on the outside you can appear to look well. Therefore you have to stand by yourself – an illness like this is trying to teach you to love who you are and making you just be you.

The soul will NEVER give up. Your soul is trying to communicate with you every minute of every day.

It is all of you, it is forever.

Your Earth version of you is such a wonderful way for souls to learn. The problem is that we make our experience here so hard and at times, traumatic, because we don't use all of the skills and information we are provided with.

Love is what we are born with. Fear is what we learn. The spiritual journey is the unlearning of fear and prejudices and the acceptance of love back in our hearts. Love is the essential reality and our purpose on Earth. To be consciously aware of it, to experience love in ourselves and others, is the meaning of life. Meaning does not lie in things it lies in us.

MARIANNE WILLIAMSON

UNCONDITIONAL LOVE

We talk about it all the time – unconditional love. It is the ultimate way to love and to be loved.

From Wikipedia, the free encyclopedia "Unconditional love – is a concept".

From Dictionary.com "un·con·di·tion·al – not limited by conditions".

Very rarely, if at all, do we love unconditionally on Earth. Not one person that I have shared this concept with likes that statement. In fact it has started some very interesting discussions. I am a mum, and I understand that feeling of 'mum-love', for me the most powerful feeling we have for our children. We would not hesitate to die for them. Dads too. My husband tells me he feels the same. That powerful knowledge that you will do anything for someone you love, that you will love them forever no matter what, is what we refer to as unconditional love. I am not taking anything away from the purity and depth of this love that we have experienced, I am just trying to open your eyes to the bigger picture, to look at this and understand this from a soul perspective.

As defined in dictionary.com, it is love that is not limited by conditions.

Can we love unconditionally? I will always tell my kids I love them unconditionally, however, I am also aware that I try to manipulate them with my words and actions to get them to do what I want because I think I know what is best for them. The fact that someone we love feels guilty about something they did or didn't do shows that the love they receive isn't unconditional. As parents we do love our children but we continuously react and respond to our children's (or anyone else we want to love) words and actions. If we try to manipulate them (even if it is for their own good) we aren't loving unconditionally. Unconditional love demands, however, that we do try to love them according to who their soul is.

From my experience of working with clients the feeling of being loved is so powerful and so craved by everyone that we will do anything to feel it. Being loved, however, really just gives us the ability to love ourselves. If people are asked what they want most in life, often the response is 'happiness'. So think about the feeling of 'happiness', it matches with being loved and allowing yourself to feel it. That is why we stop listening to ourselves and start to do what everyone else wants us to do. We want that praise, that love, that reason which means we can like ourselves. We do this from a very young age and this is why we get so lost when we are older, especially from teenage years onwards.

To love unconditionally means you are free to love that person. It also means at all times when dealing with that person you have peace. It means that you never take their power away from them or make them feel guilty, you never manipulate them to do something.

How can you do this with anyone let alone with teenagers? You see, teenagers are just the same as parents, grandparents, bosses, teachers, staff members, tradespeople, farmers or professional people. We are all trying to work out who we are. And we all do it through the approval of other people. We all feel good about ourselves only when someone else tells us it's okay.

Teenagers grow up with, "What are you going to do when you grow up?" and " Your subject choices will make or break you."

Childhood is all about your achievements as compared to other people. If you are on a desert island by yourself and you run the fastest time in the world, does it matter? No, but it does feel good to run!

To try to love unconditionally means we have to listen to the other person's soul, to help them or let them find their own being, to understand what their lessons might be, to look at all of that person – spiritual past, genetic past and Earth past.

LET'S USE TEENAGERS AS OUR EXAMPLE

Teenagers have no power, everyone else who is older holds it. They want to be loved so they try to do what everyone else wants. They can only like themselves if someone else does. They lose trust because they rely on other people to make it better, they can't hear what their souls are trying to tell them.

I have treated so many teenagers suffering from depression and who are often suicidal. There is a difference between clinical depression and depression. Clinical depression is where there is medical evidence of a chemical imbalance in the brain. Even so, remember your body has allowed you to get here because it is trying to tell you something.

Depression, however, is treatable. Depression especially in our teenagers is an epidemic. So where do you start? Firstly, they don't like themselves, when we discover that we also discover they don't know much about themselves. Their ability to like themselves is based on what everyone else thinks, on where they think they fit on the ladder or if they make the ladder at all, whether it be the social ladder or academic ladder. They also rely on other people to make it better for them. After we talk for a while I show them something – the two arm stress test. Now think about being on a deserted island all by yourself with no one else around. Now think about being able to love yourself, think about allowing yourself to be who your soul is meant to be. To their amazement they hold strong. Deep down inside they do have the ability to love themselves, they are still connected. And that is where we begin. They begin to get to know themselves. Sometimes for a while we get them to bring the deserted island along with them in their daily life. So before they react to something they think, "If I was on my deserted island would this matter?" It just helps them get their reactions to life in a better perspective while we work on finding out who they are and what they like and all the good ways that they can help themselves and love who they are, regardless of being on Earth with people. We work a lot on the statement, "I allow me to be me".

The issue of being disconnected from ourselves, not understanding ourselves and not allowing ourselves to be who we really are just continues, to all different degrees, into adult life.

PERSONAL EXAMPLE

My daughter who passed away was the one to teach me about unconditional love. For me to feel that I am a good mum I need to 'mum' my children; to love them, to feed them, to care for them. You see, I need to do things for them.

So I was struggling with the fact that, yes, I was her mum, but in no capacity does she need me anymore. I felt very distant from her because I was under the Earth feeling that I had to do things for people in order for them to love me or for me to feel I could deserve their love, or to let me feel their love.

I worked out one day that I felt distant from her because of this belief I had. She was just there, she hadn't left me, I had left her. I had to comprehend and then really understand unconditional love, and the fact that it just is.

My doing nothing ever again for her didn't matter. She just loves me! And I can just love her back!

Part 4

UNDERSTANDING WHY OUR EARTH SELVES GET LOST ON EARTH

I am not what happened to me,

I am what I choose to become.

CARL GUSTAV JUNG

POWER BUBBLES

Everyone has a power bubble. Imagine a beautiful ball of pure love and energy that lives inside you that you had when you were born. It holds the essence of us being able to love ourselves. What has happened to our power bubble? What happens is that we both give it away and we let people take it.

So what really is a power bubble? It's your feeling of self-love and deep peace, your being, your ability to really like who you are and your ability to feel peacefully empowered no matter what the circumstances are.

What happens as we go through life is our power bubble becomes dependent on what others think. So then we focus on keeping others happy to fill our power bubble. Go through some scenarios in your life. Imagine as a child being praised: good girl, or good boy, great job, you are amazing, I am so proud of you. The opinion is the other person's. The other person is giving you permission to feel good about yourself. Now we all respond to praise and I am not saying it's a bad thing, however, we can get to a point where we rely on it to believe in ourselves and then someone else or everyone else has control over our power bubble.

Parents in particular have control over our power bubbles. One look from a mum or dad can instantly diminish our bubble to nearly nothing. When we talk about how much easier it is to love ourselves on a deserted island it's because our power bubble is huge, full of self-love and acceptance for who we are.

The thing is, there isn't a need to power bubble battle. We are all born with the exact amount of power we need but we forget to rely on ours and try to use someone else's.

So why do we take energy from other peoples power bubbles? Because this is one of the first lessons we learn in life. There is a big difference between saying something to someone because you love them and saying something to someone to invoke a feeling in them, to make them feel bad, guilty, unworthy, unempowered, etc. Take, for example, your child studying year 12. She is struggling to do homework. So you say when I was in year 12 I studied for four hours a night. The balance between both your power bubbles has shifted. You now have more power while she has less power. You have confirmed that you are excellent at studying and you have confirmed that she is not very good at it. You may be trying to inspire her but you are really just power bubble battling. So how would you do it differently? Focus on her, not on you. What does her power bubble look like in relation to study? All kinds of things could help but remember she is the one that has responsibility for her power bubble. Listen first with no answers then let her come up with a plan to help herself. You could suggest ideas but let her fix it.

Think about where the power is in these two statements:
I am really proud of you.
You should be really proud of you.

The fact is that most of us have grow up with "I am really

proud of you", when we hear it, it sounds wonderful, and we begin to rely on it to help us feel good. Many clients have issues with thinking their parents aren't proud of them. However, if you really look at it, we are only giving ourselves permission to be proud of ourselves after someone else does.

Inspiring people is the only way you can help people fill their power bubbles. You see, when you inspire someone they actually take responsibility for themselves, they feel determined, stronger, they believe in themselves more and they believe they can make a difference. Think about people who have inspired you. They inspire you because they may have done something, and within you, you believe that you can do it too. Say your best friend lost 20 kilos, or your mate improved his golf handicap, instead of losing power bubble power because of it and feeling bad about yourself, use it to inspire you to change what you can in your life and see how much better you feel, how much bigger your power bubble grows.

Many times I have seen clients who were physically abused, mentally abused and/or sexually abused – one of the most horrible ways to take someone's power especially when it is so unprotected because they are so young. Years and years later if they see the abuser again, even if that person is old and can't hurt them anymore, the feeling remains the same. The person who was abused still gives the abuser their power bubble. It's because we don't know how to take it back peacefully and keep it. When working with clients we do a lot of work on this.

It is harder to protect our power bubbles as children because so many people in authority, who don't realise they were born with enough power of their own, the problem is, however, everyone else has taken parts of that person's power so they take ours.

Fathers do this to sons.

Mothers do this to daughters.

Teachers do this.

Grandparents do this.

Friends do this.

Siblings do this.

Partners do this constantly to each other.

We have all done this and we have all had it done to us.

They also give it back to us with praise.

So now we begin to need to get our power bubble filled by everyone else. We get so used to having people take our power as children that we continue to give it away as adults.

When you get a chance, stop, shut your eyes and breathe. Imagine your power bubble when you were a baby. Imagine how big and beautiful it was. Now look at your power bubble today. How big is it now? Go through all the people in your life and imagine each of them walking into a room with you one at a time. See what happens to your power bubble.

Does it shrink, do you hand it to them, do they take it?

As we get older we don't realise that people can take our power bubbles *only* if we let them.

Practise saying 'no', especially to things you know you don't want to do. 'No' doesn't need to be aggressive, it can be a decision you make that leaves you with peace. Stay in the peaceful place while you say no. The other person's reaction to your 'no' is theirs to deal with! Be aware that people try to take your power, to drain you. There really are no 'have tos' in life. We actually do have a choice, however, we find that we can't say 'no' to things because we think we are protecting our power bubble. We are trying to avoid feeling bad or feeling guilty. We are trying to avoid others thinking bad of us. Instead, if you decide NOT to visit your parents or be the team manager for your child's team, or not go to your best friend's party, then say 'no' and feel good about it.

If you say 'yes' then embrace it, enjoy every second of it. Feel inspired by saying yes. Feel your power bubble grow because you were free to say yes. You made the choice. Yes is not a 'have to', yes is a yes!

Be aware when people start trying to power bubble battle with you. Smile to yourself. Find a way inside that conversation to inspire yourself, and practise keeping your power bubble big!

While we try to teach our children all about life, our children teach us what life is all about.

ANONYMOUS

SOUL PARENT EARTH PARENT

When I die (my Earth body!) I will get to look back on MY life – not my children's, not my husband's, not anyone else's – mine. I get to look at what my soul wanted to achieve, and how I listened to and embraced that. I only look at my life. That is the only one I am responsible for. I don't get to look at anyone else's journey, that is for them to do.

HUG 'N' ROCK

As a parent we want the best for our children. Like all parents, we hope they have a good life, good friends, good education, find a beautiful partner, travel, get married, buy a house, have children and be happy.

Perfect, YES? So I do everything in my power to create this, especially when they are little. I interfere, I talk to teachers, I talk to parents and coaches. My goal is to help my children have a wonderful life. This happens and, eventually, after a long life my now-elderly child dies. They get to look back on their life and see how they went with their life lessons.

Nothing!

They were never allowed to hurt, to have to dig deep, to have to fight or rely on themselves. They missed out on learning any of the lessons that they wanted and needed.

Our job as parents and souls is to HUG 'N' ROCK. Not just our kids but everyone in our lives.

You see, all we need in life is to feel loved. If we feel loved, loveable and safe we are more likely to be who our soul wants us to be. Whenever I have had a terrible time there is nothing like a hug, a big warm soul-touching hug – with no words.

Women, you may have noticed, rock when they hug. They rock from the minute their babies are born, they hold a baby and they rock, in fact they talk about their children and if they are worried as they talk they rock. We have all been a child to a mother. We all respond to being hugged and rocked. As babies when we are in the womb we are hugged and as the mother walks we are being rocked.

You see, it is not up to us to make it better by interfering and blocking someone's lessons. It is up to us to hug 'n' rock and remind others that they are loveable and loved. To inspire them to find out, to love and accept who they really are. It's like a home-base or a battery recharger. A good hug 'n' rock allows you to find your strength to keep going.

The power of touch is healing. The power of touch reminds us without words that we are not alone. Touch is the vibration of the soul.

SOUL PARENTING

'Earth mum' versus 'Soul mum' (this relates to dads, grandparents, being a boss, a staff member, just slip in the appropriate title).

I am an 'Earth mum' which means I have a list of Earth rules that I use while being a mother. They are not written anywhere but we all know them. Actually we all unconsciously live by them. If we stop and think carefully about how we react to things, how we have reacted to things in the past, then we can start to see the influence 'Earth mum' rules have on our lives.

We want our children to have good manners, to be kind, to try hard, to do well in school, and sport. We want them to be loved and accepted by other people. We want them to 'fit in'.

Why? Underneath this is **our self-esteem** and giving **ourselves** permission to feel good about **ourselves**. However, we only allow ourselves to feel good about ourselves or to think "I am a good mother" when our children present to the world as socially acceptable and successful people, when we believe that everyone else will think "I have done a good job", or when we think other people approve of our children. That's why we encourage them to do well in everything and why we are disappointed when they don't. I know we see that especially with sports ('the pushy parent syndrome'), however, we all do it to different degrees. We have all heard or used the words "I am so disappointed in you" and we have all used or heard the words "I am so proud of you". We all know the phrase "I am happy when my kids are happy".

CLIENT EXAMPLE

Debbie's son moved out from under her roof to go and live with his dad, he was 13. She knew the care he would receive at his father's house would be much different to hers. The rules would be different and her influence on his life would be minimal. She was shattered. Firstly, because she felt rejected by her son, and secondly because it was obvious to the world that he had chosen his dad over her. She was also very angry. We had a long chat and did some work together. Remembering that life and our reaction to life is all about us – no matter how much we try to distract ourselves by blaming other people. She was angry – not at him (even though she had been taking it out on him) but at herself because she wasn't enough for him, she wanted to make it better, to make him enjoy life. When he was happy then she could like herself, she could (according to the 'Earth rules'), feel worthwhile as a mother.

So how does a 'Soul mum' work? A soul mum consciously puts aside all the 'Earth rules' and is aware of not reacting instantly because Earth mum thinks and talks first. A soul mum listens. At every possible moment her job is to step back and look at the bigger picture for this person, this soul who is in her life. She understands 'this soul', she has the privilege of helping this soul, she knows this soul has an agenda, has lessons they want to master. She learns to understand and see what her child is attracting into their life. Her job is to help her child believe in themselves and to feel loveable. To allow them the space to find who they are, to teach them to listen.

As I was talking to Debbie, we went through all the reasons she was angry and felt rejected. We discovered feeling rejected had long been a part of her life especially when her husband left her for another woman. We also went through the qualities of her son, what he had learnt so far and perhaps what he wanted to learn. She then realised that he was unable to get these next lessons from her. She understood his bigger picture, and that he now needed a different life experience – even if she knew it would be hard for him and not what her 'Earth mum' wanted him to experience. She could now see why he left, he was in fact listening to his soul. Her job in this, apart from to love him, was to work through her feelings of rejection and especially allow herself to not carry that feeling of rejection with her (I imagine it as if she was carrying a blanket) when she is with other people. And if she feels the feeling of unworthiness creep back in when she's talking to another mum – especially when they find out her son moved out – then she was to smile and remind herself that she was a 'soul mum'. This would then allow her to be a 'soul mum' when she talked to him in the future and not a mum that felt hurt, angry, rejected and abandoned. It allowed her to be free to love him instead of trying to manipulate him and make him feel guilty, instead of putting a strain on their relationship that may never be fixed.

It's your road ...

And yours alone ...

Others may walk it with you

but no one can walk it for you!

UNKNOWN

RESPONSIBILITY

Give people back their responsibility. Don't try to fix things for others.

Lots of clients I see are 'fixers'. That is they love trying to help people. The thing is though that they come to me drained and exhausted, carrying more than they can bear. The can feel very overwhelmed and unappreciated. So one of the first things we do is a visualisation. I tell them to close their eyes and think of all the people in their life they are helping and supporting at the moment. Now imagine each one of them is a storybook and put it in the bookshelf next to you. How many books are on your bookshelf?

STORY BOOK
If someone comes to talk to you about their situation and is seeking help, it is as if they are bringing their storybook to you. Their storybook is full of pictures and stories of what has happened to them so far in their life. You both sit down and read it. You then get out your pencils and draw with grey lead different pictures of what they can do. The problem is that many of us hold on to the other person's storybook, worry about them and try to make it better.

This may mean that we have a bookshelf that holds the

storybook of everyone we care about. We are 'looking after' everyone's story. The problem with this is that the other person cannot continue drawing in their storybook if they don't have it. They can't make any progress because their storybook is no longer theirs! We need to give everyone's storybook back. If we draw an outline in it we need to be okay if they take it away and rub out our outline and put in a different one. You see, they need to draw their own pictures, they need to be responsible for themselves. If they come back and they have changed the pictures we drew and we are angry at them, then:

1. We took their responsibility; we want to make it better for them.
2. We are really angry with ourselves because we can't fix it because they won't do what we want them to do.
3. We only allow ourselves to feel good when we fix someone else.

People cannot change anything unless they are in an environment where they feel safe, loved and supported. Don't keep the storybook. Instead, create an environment for them where they have the opportunity to change, where they feel loved and supported by loving and listening. A beautiful way of giving back responsibility is to **use questions.** We may know the answers but it's not our souls journey they are having, it is their own, so they need to learn how to own it. Questions are a wonderful way to do this and I promise that their souls know the answer. You are now just helping them to listen to their soul.

Identify with their feeling; don't make it better, i.e.

"Wow, that must be really difficult, I understand how you would feel like that."

Give them choices:
"What can you do about this?"
"What options do you have?"
"What ideas do you have?"

Give them the opportunity to work it out for themselves:
"How does that affect you?"
"How does that change things?"
"How can you go about that?"
"What is the worst thing that could happen?"
"How would you deal with that?"
"How would you feel?"

At NO stage in a conversation like this do you take their power bubble or their storybook or their pencils! In fact you watch them begin to find who they are and fill in their own storybooks.

The only time we ever get angry with a person is when they are not doing what we want them to do. We are angry because we can't manipulate them. Often this is with the person's best interest at heart. It makes it hard for us to realise that we are angry at ourselves, at feeling inadequate for not making it better for them. We want them to get a job, to study, to go out, to be happy. We really are angry at ourselves because we can't manipulate them. Even when we think we know it will help them, we are still trying to make them do what *we* want!

How many times do people come to us with problems where we can clearly see what they need to do, no matter how big or small the problem? Because we are outside of it we can see the answer. So, we tell the other person what we think they should do and then we feel good about ourselves because we really helped someone, only to find, the next time we see them, that they are still saying the same thing. So again we tell them what they should do. This happens again and again until we become frustrated and angry with that person, but really we feel angry at ourselves. We can't feel good about ourselves until we make someone else feel good about themselves.

Another scenario is when we jump right in to help. We physically get involved, we take responsibility for that aspect in their life, we try to fix it for them. We go clean their house from top to bottom only to find out in two months that it is just as messy. We decide we will help them lose weight only to find that you turn into a nag and there is now strain in your friendship.

I often have people come in angry and upset (especially fixers – people who have taken on responsibility for someone else's life). They say something like, I have told her/him 10 times to do this and does she listen to me? NO! Then so and so comes along and she/he thinks, "Wow that's a fantastic idea". I had already told her/him that. They are really angry that the message they had told them many times was received from someone else – they didn't get the credit for it! The person's angry response is actually about them personally. Everything is all about you personally, the fixer in this case. The fixer can only feel good about themselves when they are 'helping' other people. Actually, very often the same answer has been right there in front of them all along. It has been said in different angel books I have read. That if you hear something three times then it is a message for you. It is very hard sometimes for the fixer to find delight in the fact that this person had 'got it', they understand, they can move forward. Especially when the fixer doesn't get the credit for helping.

If you are a fixer it helps if you can imagine it this way. It is like you put on a super hero suit on when someone is in need. You feel and become so empowered nothing can stop you. The problem is that you become responsible for everyone else's life and decisions and outcomes that you lose focus of yourself. However feeling like a super hero leaves you feeling empowered until the person you are fixing doesn't do what you want! They can't do what you want because their life is all about them (not you) they need to learn and understand things for themselves. So here's a thought: Instead of being everyone else's super hero, help them find their own super hero suit, by empowering them to make it better for themselves. Yes, everyone has their own super hero suit, different colours, different logos, different looks. But everyone's super hero suit is perfect for them. By asking questions and reminding them to empower themselves, and you not taking on responsibility to take over and make it better you can really help them. One day you might help them to help themselves find their mask, the next their lycra outfit, the next their undies for the outside of their costume! And maybe even their cape. We really need to inspire, encourage and hug 'n' rock but not take over.

I have used this analogy with lots of the children I see and they love it. We actually discuss and design what their super hero suit will look like. When they feel anxious or scared they can imagine themselves in their custom self-made super hero suit that they created. They then don't need to rely on anyone else to make it better for them, they can problem solve it for themselves; they get to keep their power. It works with any age.

Remember the only person's soul to-do list we look back on when we die is our own.

So keep your bookshelf with the most important book on it yours! When you are talking to people about their problems remember to empower them, and be delighted for them no matter who helps or inspires them and make sure they take their storybook and their super hero suit with them!

If nothing ever changed there'd be no butterflies.

UNKNOWN

Change is the essence of life ...

Be willing to surrender what you are for what you could become.

UNKNOWN

CHANGE

There are two guarantees in life, one is death, the other is change. Change can instantly disempower people. They feel insecure, they can become angry or anxious. People instantly lose their feeling of 'safe' or their feeling of 'free'. Yet change continually happens in life. We constantly deal with change on a daily basis and we still try to avoid it. Change is really just another opportunity to have a life experience.

VEGEMITE TOAST

A beautiful mum came in one day struggling with the fact that her children weren't coping. Her children were four and six and she had gone back to work on a Saturday. She had been at home raising them for six years, so it was a big change for them all. Her husband was caring for them on Saturdays and he was struggling too, as the kids kept saying he did everything differently to mum.

She was talking about Vegemite toast!
They both would not eat the Vegemite toast he made for them on Saturday mornings because it was not the same as mum did it! We spoke about this for a while as she was thinking about leaving work and staying at home.

Change is guaranteed in life. It will always happen, in

every aspect of our life. Her children were experiencing big change for the first time in their lives. She had two choices:
- She could leave work and they would feel secure and safe again and she could protect them from change as long as she could. Then, at 18, they could go out into the world and be confronted by change in a not-so-loving and supportive environment, or
- She could continue working knowing she was teaching them about change, leaving them in a place where they were loved and cared for, safe and looked after – even if it was different to what they were used to.

She stayed at work.

Being resistant to change blocks the flow of life. Life still happens but it makes it harder for everyone. Say you are too scared to change jobs. Then the person who is perfect for the job you are doing now doesn't get the opportunity to do that job. Or find their new partner, or new house or you may never find that you enjoy something you have never tried before.

We block change because of fear but what are we scared of – success or failure? If we fail have we really failed? Yes, if we put our energy and thoughts into what we think other people think. But if we bring it back to just ourselves didn't we just have a life experience? Didn't going through that experience teach us something? Didn't that experience help us to get to know ourselves better? Isn't that why we are here?

If we succeed – well imagine that. Not from the perspective of succeeding in other people's eyes because then all of our energy is there. We don't want to feel what their success is. You want to feel what your success feels like, to have inspired yourself.

Imagine if we can let go of the 'what everyone else thinks' way of thinking from all aspects in our being. People say all the time to me, "I don't care what everyone else thinks". I understand that statement but if we really look at the way we live, how we block ourselves and how we resist change then we are still being influenced by what everyone else thinks whether it be conscious on not. We live and react from our subconscious and all our belief systems that have been created. We have to be aware of this every second of our day. Not so we can ignore it but so we can embrace it as part of us and not let it block us. It's like giving a nod to the neighbour across the road. We just give a nod, a smile within us, to acknowledge the 'what everyone else thinks' moment that passed through.

If we see change as an adventure, an opportunity for our souls to teach us new things, to show us all the possibilities that life has to offer, imagine how excited we would be for change to happen. Imagine just how good our lives could be.

Worrying does not empty tomorrow of its troubles ... it empties today of its strength.

CORRI TEN BOOM

WORRYING ABOUT THINGS

We spend so much of our energy worrying. People will say, "Oh, I am a worrier." They spend their day worrying about all sorts of things: family, friends, what's happening with the world. In fact the more they worry the more unsafe they feel. Unsafe feelings lead to anxiety. I have seen more and more anxiety in the world, and more children are coming to see me with anxiety.

So what can we do about this? Death, especially for children, is a huge worry. I remember as a child, being worried that one of my parents would die. As a parent we worry that our children will be okay. Our biggest fear is that one of them will die.

Much of what happens in life we can't change, many things we can't control, yet worrying can take over our lives.

There is one simple rule, WORRY ABOUT THE THINGS YOU CAN CHANGE, and only that. Can you worry about getting a job? Of course, you can change that. Can you worry about your maths? Yes, you can change that too. Can you worry about how you communicate with your partner or children? Again, yes.

Can you worry that someone might die? Can't change it. Can you worry if your partner will get a job? You can't change that, only he/she can. Can you worry that your child will do okay at school? Can you worry that the sun will shine on a particular day? Can you worry if your train will be cancelled or not? You can't change any of those situations either.

It doesn't mean that worry is not real. It is very real but, underneath, worry is the feeling of not being safe and secure, of not being able to control things how we want. Worry stops us from listening and being ourselves. In fact worrying can change us so much that we don't realise we are manipulating ourselves, especially if we are scared that someone will leave us. We try so hard to become the person we think they want us to be that we lose ourselves completely.

So what can we do? How can we not worry? Think about what worries you. If you can change it and still be yourself, stop worrying and work out a plan for change. Talk to people to help give you ideas, listen to what you think is right. Find your power bubble. Trust yourself and then change it. Take a risk – ask yourself, "If I change this, what is the worst that can happen?" Once you identify the worst thing it may not seem so bad, you can be okay. In fact it gives you back your power and a feeling of control. This control is a peaceful control not an aggressive control.

Peaceful control has a base of trust. The feeling of peace comes because, no matter what happens, you understand that the outcome will be okay, it will be what is meant to be for you. This helps you learn and understand everything about yourself. It doesn't mean that you should now sit back and wait for life with no goals or determination, it means that you can go through life striving for the next step, that you use life experiences as stepping stones. You can always listen and be open to working out what you are learning while you are journeying.

Aggressive control happens when you set your sights on an outcome or a goal and let nothing get in your way. You ignore the people you meet on your path who could have helped you change your life and blindly strive for what it is you want. Often this is when big life-changing incidents happen to try to get you back on track to your soul path. Or you make it to where you want to be and you still don't feel good.

If there is nothing you can do to change it, we have to work out a way for you to stop giving your energy to it, a way for you to let it go. This often comes down to your personal belief systems. When I am working with clients, both adults and children, we talk about different scenarios.

Many people have heard of guardian angels. We chat about a guardian angel that has been with you since you were conceived whose task is to look after and protect you. This resonates well with some people.

At other times we look at individual angels. These are angels who are waiting to help but are unable to do so unless they are asked. People talk about carpark angels (ask the carpark angel to help you with finding a carpark before you leave for the shops – it really works!). There are angels for everything, for healing, for studying, for communication, for awakening, for depression. Whatever you are worried about will have an angel. As a last resort you could go the wildcard angel and that should cover everything! You can then invoke, say a prayer, or just ask for that angel to help, or be with that person. I know some mothers who imagine themselves walking up and just dumping their child in the angel's arms and saying "Fix this!"

When my son was little I remember explaining this concept to him. The next morning I remember him telling me he had had a busy night directing angels to different people to look after. They are really bored mum, he said, all they do is play cards, they have nothing else to do because no one ever asks them to help.

Other people choose to use departed loved ones – say a grandparent or parent. They felt on Earth a closer connection to them so it's easier for them to trust. You can actually have one deceased parent looking after all of your 18 grandchildren at the same time. You see, in heaven we are not confined to a body – we are energy. That means we can be in more than one place and help more than one person at a time. It's important that we realise this. I have had some people say, "My mum died but I think my brother needs her more, so I don't bother her."

Please bother her!

She can't help unless she is asked and then she will welcome helping all of you.

CLIENT EXAMPLE

Another interesting thing that came up with a client was that in the final stages of her dad's life, he had suffered from Alzheimer's, so the roles in the relationship had changed. She had become the carer and he had become childlike and unreliable due to his illness. She was sad because she was scared she would always remember him this way even after he died and that he could never be someone she relied on in life again. When people die, no matter how old, how sick, or how incapacitated they are when they die, they are free of all of that – their limited bodies do not go with them. They are perfectly able to love and look after you and your worries. You just have to ask! They don't take Earth emotions with them. They see the bigger picture, they are aware of what your soul is trying to achieve.

Say you never got on with a parent – remember that they may well have been your greatest teacher. They came here to teach you and make it hard for you so that you could learn what it was your soul wanted.

Their soul loves you the most!

Souls can't take on earthbound emotions of anger, hurt and disappointment. They can feel only the heaven emotions, such as peace, love, joy and understanding.

I know this is hard to get your head around, but, when it finally sinks in, the freedom you are able to feel is wonderful.

CLIENT EXAMPLE

The grandmother of one little girl I was seeing had passed away while minding the little girl. As the little girl was there and she saw her grandma die, her ability to feel safe was challenged, perhaps so much that this will be a life lesson for her. We had done a lot of work clearing this for her and some years later she came back. Her mother had been very sick and she was suffering with bad anxiety. We went through her awareness that people die, just right there and it's the end. Her fear was not just what if, but very real because she had lived through this.

I can never change this for her. It is a life experience with many lessons attached. However, I can help her find her feeling of being safe again. So, after a balance, we then did a meditation where she asked her grandma in. Her grandma had made a big basket for her to hold all the worries that she can't change. Now, every night before she goes to sleep she visits her grandma and puts her worries in the basket.

Children can worry about all sorts of things. Toilet training can be scary, the dark is scary, school can be scary, bed time can be scary. Often children won't go to sleep in their beds unless mum or dad sits with them. I have teenagers that I see that still sleep with mum. I see many parents and children together for similar issues to these above. Lots of children resort to saying they are sick, or actually becoming sick to make sure a parent stays with them. So how do we go about dealing with these issues? Parents are 'fixers'. It does feel wonderful to know that we can help our child feel safe, and not be scared and as a parent we love that our children need us, it feeds our self worth. However, we often don't realise that by us (the parent) fixing what is worrying the child means that because we make it all better, we then have all the power and the child can't problem solve or rely on themselves to make it better. In these sessions I do with parents and children after we clear any blocks or anxiety, we then come up with lots of ideas to help the children learn to make it better for themselves, and different things they can try. Some of these ideas include: swap teddy bears with mum or dad, play music, play a guided kids meditation, sleep with the dog, count backwards, say a prayer to a grandparent or an angel, imagine themselves in a super hero suit, imagine themselves in a coloured bubble, investigate how a toilet works, put a happy face on a ping pong ball and name it, then put him in the toilet bowl as their friend, the list is endless. However, everything on this list helps the children keep their power, build on their skills of relying on themselves, problem solve and to self love.

Often we can't change things but we still need to do things which help us feel safe, which help us keep our power. We can't rely on other people to do this for us, it must be done by us.

Trust and the ability to trust has a big part in being able to let go of worrying.

Your ability to relax is in direct proportion to your ability to trust life.

UNKNOWN

TRUST

There are two types of Trust – Earth Trust and Universe Trust.

The problem is, we base all of our understanding of trust on Earth trust. Earth trust, as we all have experienced at one time or another, is very unreliable. We trust that our brother will cover for us if we sneak out. We trust that our mother will remember to pick up our dress, or our wife the dry-cleaning. We trust that dad will come to our performance. We trust our friends will stick up for us. We trust our partner won't cheat on us. In fact by the time we reach adulthood we would have had our trust broken hundreds of times.

So time and time again our ability to trust is destroyed. Now we can allow ourselves to look at life with a negative attitude. Nothing good ever happens to me. I am unlucky. Nothing goes right for me. Everyone lies. No one is ever there for me. Everyone just let's me down. You can end up feeling like "what is the point, I hate my life".

The problem with Earth trust is that you are guaranteed lots of times to be let down. Everyone's life is actually all about them. People don't intentionally try to break someone's trust it just happens. They respond to a situation and someone else gets hurt. Even if your dad didn't make it to your performance because he was a fireman and was saving someone's life, it doesn't matter, in the big picture your trust was still broken. We can try and justify it and tell ourselves that it's okay, he didn't mean it, but a fact is still a fact, your trust was broken.

The trust I am talking about that can really help you find your peace is any or all of the following: universal trust, trust in your higher self, trust in angels, trust in God, trust in your soul self. You see, you made a plan before you came here on what you wanted to learn. YOU MADE IT, no one else made it. In fact no one else actually has a clue what your plan is all about. So let's re-focus and try and see where this fits into your life so far.

In primary school you were put in a class that you didn't want to be in and you met the new girl who is still your best friend today. You missed out on the job you really wanted and you found out the company closed two months later. You missed out on your perfect house at the auction which would have given you a huge mortgage and the next month your husband left. The girl you so desperately wanted to go out with went out with your best mate and then the girl of your dreams walks into your life. You missed the qualifying time for the state titles by 0.01 of a second so you work even harder and make the team at the last minute because someone falls ill.

There are over 200 individual reasons why people did not go to work on September 11. None of the reasons are particularly good and they may have even been really annoyed at the time. However, none of those people died that day.

Your soul self has your ultimate best interest at heart. Your soul self is going to, at all costs, help you achieve what you want to achieve. Your soul self is your soul mate and your soul self can and does love you unconditionally. The problem is that we pre-decide what we want to happen. What we know (without knowing the bigger picture) or think we know will make us happy. Our focus stays stuck on what we want so when it doesn't happen, we become disillusioned and lost and then we focus on what we don't have instead of the opportunities before us. Instead of finding peace in the situation we are angry and very much blocked.

It doesn't mean you shouldn't have goals and dreams, by all means, they are so important. Goals and dreams help us and make us move forward. Just remember to listen to life and life's opportunities while you do move forward. Have your outcome in mind but also don't be shattered if it doesn't turn out the way you planned it. Life will often have different plans for us. Trust!

Trust – real trust – must be done with no outcome.

When you ask for help from the universe, God, angels, guides, loved ones in heaven, you must simply ask for **help**, clear your mind in how you think or what you think that help should be. This is really hard when it comes to asking for help for the people we love but remember to trust that their soul, too, has their best interest at heart.

You might want your child to try harder at school, so you ask a deceased loved one or angel to help them to focus on their study. If he did it your way he may never become the builder he was meant to be, he may then not meet his future wife, or your daughter may never have met the teacher that she met at TAFE who inspired her to teach after she dropped out of her other school, etc.

By all means ask, but don't have your outcome in mind. Sometimes things happen for a reason and it's not until we look back on things that we can understand or see the bigger picture.

I assure you, though, that if you practise trusting, when you do, the feeling of peace that you will have all day every day is like being in Heaven on Earth.

The book *The Celestine Prophecy* by James Redfield, talks about life and if there are coincidences or 'meant to bes'.

CLIENT EXAMPLE

Jane had been coming to see me for a while. We had worked out that her issue was trust. She was attracting things into her life that were all trust confronting issues. On this particular day she was extremely stressed as she had been trying to sell her house for some time. We talked again about things either being in your control or not. Meaning that when you can't change something you can't worry about it, you need to 'ask' for help.

Help from an angel, she said was what she had been asking. Every weekend for the past few months she had been asking the angels to sell her house. She was very frustrated and disillusioned as this still hadn't happened. She was unable to make the next house repayment, so she was in a pretty bad way.

I reminded her that it was fantastic that she was asking for help, I also reminded her that she was focusing on the outcome. Maybe the angels had other plans for her and her house, or maybe the people meant to buy her house were blocked for some reason. She needed to ask for help, just help, no outcome.

She then went through the process of finding where the feeling was in her body of no trust, frustration, etc. She gave this a colour and imagined being able to put this colour in a box. She then gave this box to the angels saying, "Please fix this situation I am in, please help me as you can see the bigger picture. Please also help me to trust that it will be okay."

Even though her situation hadn't changed she felt much better. She left with a mantra to help her not to 'take back' her worry and instead be able to leave it with the angels.

"I don't have to worry about this situation, the angels have got it." Every time she felt worried again she just needed to say this.

Two days later she won a car, which she sold and used some of it to make the next few house repayments and clear her backlog of bills!

One month later she sold the house, and found and bought the perfect house for herself!

CLIENT EXAMPLE

This is one of my favourite big picture stories!

It started off as a normal night. A client had cancelled that evening and another client rang to see if she could move her appointment from next week to tonight. Perfect, I thought, that works.

Client one comes in. "How was your month?" I asked. My client looks up. "Not that good," she said. "My sister died." She then explained her story and why she was so distressed. Her sister had been feeling unwell all day. Her husband had wanted to take her to the hospital but she refused. Finally she had given in and at 2.00 a.m. he had driven her to the local hospital. When she got out of the car she was struggling to walk. As she got half way across the car park she collapsed. He ran in to get help and while he was getting help she passed away. She was quite distressed that her sister has passed away in the car park all by herself. We talked, did a kinesiology balance and she left.

Client two comes in. The client that had called to move her appointment forward. "How have you been?" I asked. "Distressed," she said. "Let me tell you about my Friday night." And she too explained her story to me. Her mum lives with her and suffers from diabetes. Her mum had gone out with a friend that day to a shopping centre. They decided to eat lunch so they went to the food mall and had a bite to eat. Around midnight her mum had become quite ill with food poisoning. Because her mum was a diabetic she rang the help line nurse on call. The help line suggested she call an ambulance as her mum was quite ill, so she called an ambulance. She then followed the ambulance into the local hospital. As she parked her car she noticed a couple walking across the car park. The woman seemed to be struggling. She saw the woman collapse and the husband run in to get help. So she ran across to the woman's side. She was quite distraught because the woman had died right there in front of her while holding her hand. The husband had thought she was one of the nurses.

So many many things had to fall into place for her sister to find out she didn't die by herself. I love this example. Trust, there is a bigger picture.

I choose to live by choice, not by chance,

to make changes, not excuses;

to be motivated and not manipulated;

to be useful, not used.

I choose self-esteem, not self-pity;

to listen to my inner voice,

not the random opinions of others.

ZERO DEAN

GUILT

GUILT – The most powerful, destructive way to be manipulated or manipulate someone else.

Guilt works a lot with power bubbles. To avoid the feeling of guilt, we will always give our power away. Guilt is not an emotion. Guilt is a choice.

So many clients say, "My parents make me feel guilty, in fact, anyone can make me feel guilty. Avoiding guilt and feeling guilty rules my life!" There is an art to manipulating people and parents have it down pat with their children. It all starts in childhood.

Whenever you think you feel guilty, be aware that you are still choosing to feel guilty. Ask yourself am I embracing the Earth emotions of "I am inadequate, unworthy, unlovable", etc., if I DON'T do whatever it is that I am being manipulated to do. Test it, "Can I say 'No'?" If not, why can't I? If you answer it is because I feel guilty, then you are letting yourself be manipulated.

I understand some very powerful guilt trips can be played. However, if you keep accepting it and doing whatever it is because you are responding to guilt, then it can't change. You are the only one who can change the impact guilt will have on your life and how you will be manipulated by it. Also, be aware of how you try to shame others into things. If you were brought up with guilt then you will certainly use guilt to manipulate those around you.

If you continue to respond by doing things to avoid feeling guilty then nothing can change. You will never be free. You will never have peace.

Here is the secret:

Guilt is **a creative learning opportunity for the other person involved!**

What do I mean by this? Instead of feeling guilty, which if you really think about it only makes you feel bad, instead look at it as an opportunity to teach. It's really about teaching the person that **you think** you have let down (hence your feeling of guilt). Change your thinking around. They now get a learning opportunity. They have to try something else, ask someone else or find a solution to a situation all by themselves. Say you couldn't take your grandmother to the doctor. She either needs to ask another person, get a taxi or change her appointment and wait until you can do it. It's just a fact. You don't need to feel bad. You just choose to feel bad because you have gone to the Earth rules and think you should be able to do everything and still be happy. Say you feel guilty because you can't put your kids to bed twice a week because you work – you can't change that either. Rejoice in the fact that you empower someone else to do it, maybe your spouse or a grandparent. You give them an opportunity to spend some quality time with your children.

PERSONAL EXAMPLE

All of our family was out one day in two different cars, in two different places. One of our daughters was at a friend's house. Both of us (parents) thought the other one was picking her up. Needless to say neither of us did. The lady whose house she was at had to go out so she dropped our daughter home and left. No one was home, it was dark and she was scared so she went to the neighbours and knocked on the door and waited there until someone came home.

Now I have two choices. I can feel really guilty and beat myself up. This doesn't help anyone, I hate myself more and I take on the Earth emotions, "OMG what will other people think? I am so inadequate as a parent!"

OR

I can be full of joy.

She had had a creative learning experience. She got to problem solve. She learnt a beautiful life lesson of how she can make things better for herself. She now has something to refer to for the rest of her life on how she can make things better. She created a self-empowering pattern!

So I can love me. I gave my child a wonderful learning opportunity!

Love is the ability and the willingness to allow those that you care for to be what they choose for themselves without any insistence that they satisfy you.

DR WAYNE DWYER

REMOVING GUILT FROM YOUR LIFE

People's reactions to you no longer allowing yourself to be manipulated by guilt can get very interesting.

Creating learning opportunities can get a little messy for a while. You see, people don't want to change, they want things to stay the same way, even if it means they don't learn and are avoiding what it is that their soul is trying to learn. Behind trying to make you feel guilty there is a feeling, and that feeling will be all about the other person. It might be that if all of my children don't show up to a function then people might think we are not a close family. Or if I don't have people around me I don't know how to feel loved. Sometimes it's not easy to see but there is always a feeling that is causing the person who you are dealing with to try to make you feel guilty. That's why things can get messy because underneath it all you are putting the person trying to make you feel guilty way out of their comfort zone. If you try to stop yourself being manipulated by guilt, then the person you are dealing with is likely to throw everything at you.

"You are ungrateful!"

"How could you?"

"You are so selfish!" etc.

What they are really doing is having an adult version of

a two-year-old tantrum and instead of banging their fists on the floor to manipulate you (because it looks really odd when a 30-year-old sprawls themselves across the floor!) they are now using words that they have used on you before which they know work to get what they want. If you give in to a child, next time they will repeat the tantrum because it worked and they got what they wanted. Parents and everyone else in your life, even bosses, do the same.

If your two-year-old had an absolute all out tantrum because they wanted a chocolate frog at 9.00 in the morning, you would probably just stand there and watch and say, "Are you done?" Or you would walk away and wait until they had got the tantrum out of their system, but you wouldn't give in to it. Why then can we not use the same logic when dealing with adults.

When changing the rules, people get elaborate with their tantrums. The words they use are big words to try to manipulate you. Try to look at this situation a different way. Don't listen to their words, listen to their souls. They might just be saying things like, "But I am scared you won't visit me", or "I don't think I am loveable so I am trying to make you love me", or "What will other people think? How will I be judged?"

Treat their outbursts the same as you would a two-year-old tantrum. You can even think, "Are you done?" Step back and realise what is really happening. See the bigger picture. This should help you not react. Still leave them with love. While you watch them remember you are teaching them, you are giving them a creative learning opportunity. Their tantrum will end when they realise you won't be manipulated. Then you have kept your power bubble, and eventually real communication can begin.

If you do react to the tantrum then it is because part of you believes that they are saying, "You need to deal with this." Understand what it is that lets you be manipulated. Maybe you allow yourself to be manipulated because you are scared that your partner might leave. Or that you might be written out of a will. Or your child will walk out. Or you will get fired. Do your questions."What is the worst thing that could happen? Am I allowing myself truly to be myself with this person or in this situation?" It doesn't mean you have to leave them either, it just means you have to embrace and empower yourself and provide an opportunity for learning where there is love and support.

It is not up to you to make it better for them or anyone. They have to make it better for themselves, they have to understand the real reason behind their tantrum, and they can't do that unless you stop allowing yourself to feel guilty. If you are not happy with a situation, then you have the power to change it and in the process you give others a learning opportunity.

When you judge another,

you do not define them,

you define yourself.

DR WAYNE DWYER

RAFFLE TICKETS!

We use words constantly to try to manipulate people to do what we want them to do. If you really look at your conversations or even listen in to other people's conversations you will see how much we all do this.

Every single minute of the day, in every single conversation, raffle tickets are being passed between people!

By 'raffle tickets' I mean that with my choice of words, I am tearing off a raffle ticket to give to you. On that raffle ticket is a feeling. I give you that raffle ticket to try to make you feel what I want you to feel. You can feel this only if you accept the ticket. Let me use some examples – guilt is used the most!

"I worked so hard all day and I'm so exhausted and yet you can't even put the dishes away."

"I drove my son to school with my last $5 of petrol in the car."

"If you don't try harder at school, you will end up as a bum on the dole."

"I sit here all day long and no one comes to visit me."

"Your sister never does that."

"Oh, she's not sitting up yet – Jamie's already walking."

"Your kids go to sleep at 10.30 p.m. Gosh, mine are asleep by 7.00 p.m."

"You let your kids run around with no shoes."

"Jane's husband just got a $5,000 pay rise."

Now we have a choice whether we take this ticket or not.

If I say to you that the sky is really green today, or that I just saw a flock of dogs fly by, or you have blonde hair and I say what lovely dark hair you have, it doesn't make sense does it? It can't resonate with you because there is not one part of you that believes it. So we can only be made to feel something if part of us already believes it, if part of us already feels inadequate, or a failure, or unworthy. We can feel these feelings only when we compare ourselves to other people. If we turn our ladder sideways and begin to be us, be who our soul is meant to be, then we won't be accepting tickets from other people.

People give you a ticket because it makes them feel better about themselves – it makes them feel higher up their ladder than you.

The easiest way to deal with raffle tickets, to not take them, and to leave them with the other person, is to agree.

"Your kids go to sleep at 10.30 p.m! Gosh, mine are asleep by 7.00 p.m." If you turn your ladder sideways, you can then respond, "I know it's wonderful for me that mine go to sleep at 10.30 p.m. It's my favourite time of the day. We all get to snuggle, play games, read books and have cuddles. I just love it." You give the feeling ticket back to them.

You are at a function and someone who never misses a function says, "Oh well, it's so nice to see you here. You haven't been to a function in ages!" It is said in a way to put you down and you reply, "Yes isn't it wonderful! I had nothing on today. It was so nice to see everyone!" Then they still have the ticket.

They have tried to put you down to make them feel better about themselves, but it's as if you can't even tell they are trying to put you down, you embraced their statement and gently returned the ticket to them! You will find very quickly when you don't take people's tickets and stop feeling bad about yourself (so they can feel good about themselves), that they will stop trying to give you tickets because you stopped taking them and they will move on to someone else in the hope that the new person will take the ticket.

Part 5

UNDERSTANDING OUR EARTH SELVES ON EARTH

I am in competition with no one. I run my own race. I have no desire to play the game of being better than anyone, in any way, shape or form. I just aim to improve, to be better than I was before. That's me and I am free.

UNKNOWN

EXPECTATIONS

We are given everything in our life on a daily basis to help us understand ourselves. The problem is that from a very early age we are taught not to feel, not to look at the relevance of what is going on in our lives. We are taught not to listen to our bodies, and we are taught to focus on what the Earth rules are. Then we begin a life of constantly comparing ourselves to others. From here we can never feel good enough, we can never be our true selves, we can never have peace.

Expectations are things imposed upon us by:
- Ourselves
- Other people
- Society
- Media
- Family
- Work
- School (and the list will keep going).

They impose 'have tos' on us like:
- Clean house/room
- Be a great family member
- Make sure everyone else is happy
- Washing, ironing, gardening, doing the shopping

- A grades at school, university degree
- Good paying job, family is provided for
- Fit and healthy (and boy does this list go on).

There is a different list of expectations for a mother, father, brother, sister, daughter, son, extended family member, friends, students, workers and bosses, the older we get the more roles we play in life, the more expectations we feel we have to live up to.

We bring all these expectations into our life. Achieving these expectations relates directly to our ability to love ourselves.

Imagine we are born and the path ahead of us is straight. We know what our souls want to achieve. Then as we get older we start adopting expectations. Expectations really can't be put upon us, we actually invite them in. The more of them we invite in the less likely we are to be free to be ourselves. They are allowed to stay if we use them only to inspire us, however, if we use them as the only way to like ourselves then they will block who we were meant to be.

At birth our path is straight. Each expectation is like a curve that is added to our path. We travel down this path constantly being diverted. We can even go the wrong way for a while. Our path now becomes a maze, at times leaving us feeling lost because we can't see ahead past all the twists and turns. The more expectations we can be free from, the more our path will straighten out.

I am allowed truly to love myself (in my Earth mind) when: my kids are happy and well looked after, my husband is happy and well looked after, washing is done, ironing is done, house is clean, pantry stocked, everyone fed, seen my parents, on top of things at work, my staff are happy, caught up with different friends who need me and the list goes on and on. Familiar to anyone? My list of what I should accomplish in a day is so big I can't achieve it anymore! That's why the older we get the harder it is to feel good about ourselves.

What happens is that we play 'roles' in our lives. Each role we adopt comes with a list of expectations. We all have an idea of what a 'good' mother, father, wife, husband, child, boss, worker, student should be. We tap into the 'list' of qualities we think these people should have and never feel good enough because we can't live up to all the qualities that are on that list. The problem is we compare ourselves to that list without ever really trying to understand ourselves.

My list used to be like a hotel, except I had put all of my expectations for myself on the top floor – the penthouse suite! The older I became however, the more I realised my hotel only had an express elevator that went straight to the top floor!

So I had to renovate my hotel! Instead of all my goals being on the top floor I have placed all of them on an individual floor. I also fixed my elevator – it now goes up and down and stops at all floors! I don't have to wait to reach the top before I allow me to love me, I don't have to achieve the impossible. I can get one or two things done and be okay when my daily plans change and still be able to like myself. In fact on the bottom floor I have 'I got up!' So I can love myself today.

We can't get rid of the lists because they are secretly ingrained in us. We can, however, change how we feel. We can consciously allow ourselves to feel good even if we achieve only one or two things. Having what I call movable expectations also then allows you to listen to life better. Say your plan was to get up early, wash the car and do some shopping, your friend rings distraught and you drop everything to be with them. Then at the end of the day instead of feeling bad because you didn't get done what you wanted, you can be delighted in yourself because you embraced being a friend today. In fact, this way we get to listen more to life and what our soul wants.

I picture it a little like this in my head: I am walking along pushing my wheelbarrow. As my day goes along I try to put more and more things in my wheelbarrow until it is overflowing and balanced precariously. Years ago when something fell off I would stop to pick it up and put it back on. Now I just glance at it and think, oh, that's okay, mustn't be meant to do that today!

VCE NO MARKS

Everybody is a genius. But if you judge a fish by its ability to climb a tree, it will live its whole life believing that it is stupid.

Albert Einstein

I see many very stressed year 11 and year 12 students. I say to them all, I want you to go through year 11 and 12 and NOT EVER know any marks that you get. They look at me dumbfounded! Then I say "imagine if you went through the next two years trying your hardest, working to your capability, getting positive feedback on what you had done well and encouragement for what you could expand on in your learning. How would your stress be?" Most of them say "GONE".

Let's look at year 11 and 12. Everything is about marks. You receive results for assignments, tests, SACs. You look straight at your mark and instantly place yourself on the ladder. The higher up you get the more you can love yourself. Your friends in the class ask what you got. Your parents, teachers, do the same. All your marks get compared to every other child in the state.

It's because we are programmed to find our ability to love ourselves by comparing ourselves to other people. This means we are taking our emotions from the Earth emotion pool. It's a very dangerous thing to do if we only take our emotions from here. If we do take our self-love and self-worth from this pool then we only get it by comparing ourselves to others. This means that we now open ourselves up to feelings of inadequacy, unworthiness, guilt, depression. Our ability to love ourselves now comes from 'expectations' that we should achieve at work, school, or home.

So how can you get through VCE unscathed and not damaged by marks? I tell all my clients, I know the marks won't go but you can change how you feel about them by not dipping in to the Earth emotion pool. Use them as something that can only inspire you. Only compare yourself to you. Your life will work itself out. You will follow your correct path if you are free from expectations that put curves in your path. You also then get to really like yourself and be full of peace on the way.

I know two self-made millionaires who both left school at year 10 because they were struggling, but they didn't embrace other people's expectations, they followed what made them feel good!

Everything you do is based on the choices you make. It's not your parents, your past relationships, your job, the economy, the weather, an argument or your age that is to blame. You and only you are responsible for every decision and choice you make. Period.

UNKNOWN

BLAME

Blame – a way to stay stuck in something.

Why we can't move forward – Blame.

Too often we blame other people or say, "My God they have issues!" We feel powerless to change anything, we become a victim, stuck in the same pattern. Blame just means I give my power away to someone else.

Blaming others is very dangerous and extremely debilitating, but it is also the easiest way not to look at things you need to examine. "It's not my fault." There's a statement! Blame means that we wash our hands of all responsibility, that we embrace being a victim and that we get stuck. We settle in a place and then we wait for someone else to make it better. The problem is, no one can ever make it better the way we need it to be made better. We are the only ones who can do this!

People can spend most of their lives in this place and that can be very draining on other people, especially the 'fixers', those who try to make it better for everyone else. Eventually what happens is that the blaming person is so determined to stay there that the fix-it person moves on (because they can't fix it) and a new fix-it person comes along and tries. All this does is continue to keep people stuck in blaming and stuck in the fix-it mode.

Blaming others or feeling like a victim, most often starts in childhood. Most children are told what to do. If a child is stuck in a house where there is violence or mental illness, or their parents go through a divorce, or a parent is very controlling, or a child is bullied, the child can't change any of this since they are at the mercy of the people around them and the choices that these people make.

Children often make it to adulthood feeling very much like a victim. They avoid or rebel against authority and continue this process throughout their adult life. Alternatively, they may have been living in a fight–flight situation which in kinesiology we call an 'adrenal state'. They survive on adrenalin. At every turn they are ready, pumped up, like they have braced themselves, so life becomes like a fight for them. They make it into adulthood exhausted. They can't turn off, can't sleep. They can't thrive in life, things keep going wrong and they feel powerless.

Children who make it through circumstances like these and move on into adulthood often become what we label as 'control freaks'. It's because they can feel safe only when they are in control, because life for them lost credibility, they lost trust. The only person they now trust is themselves, so they shut themselves down. They will see life experiences as bad things that keep happening to them instead of as opportunities to find out who they are.

So many people are stuck in this blame or victim state. They can't find themselves. They are very personally unempowered. They struggle with achieving anything in their lives. They may not even have a job. Or they take on responsibility that's not theirs. They become responsible for making sure everything is okay in everyone else's lives. They focus on fixing everything in other people's lives, but within themselves they are a mess – drained, lost, unappreciated. They feel nothing they do is ever good enough. They can have anxiety, depression, relationship issues. They are unable to love themselves. When really they were just never taught to listen to life, to embrace their life experiences, to learn to understand themselves.

Blame means nothing can change in our lives. Blame means we are blind to the big picture. We even have a victim ladder, 'Oh, that happened to you', so we lower our expectations of that person which in turn helps them to lower their expectations. If we put down what happened to us and work out what we were trying to learn (with no regard to the other people or situation) then we can begin to move forward and be free. Your life is all about understanding you, being responsible for you not anyone else.

I didn't change I just woke up.

UNKNOWN

CREATING THE SAME PATTERN

Life's struggles are opportunities.

Life gives us hints. Understand that we create our own situations, we allow this to happen. People continuously create the same pattern. Or continuously find themselves in the same situation. Sometimes they can be quite destructive patterns.

Clients come in saying, "My mother suffered from a mental illness, and now so does my husband, or child. Why do I keep having to deal with this?"

Or you finally make it out of an abusive home only to find you have walked into an abusive marriage!

Or, even more simply, you find your boss undermines you so you change jobs to find your next boss also undermines you.

Or every partner you have ever had has cheated on you. If this is you, instead of feeling very unlucky, or asking why this keeps happening to me, turn it around and think about what you are trying to learn. Be excited because you just worked out a massive hint as to your lessons and why you are here. Try to understand your life from your soul's perspective and what you really want for yourself. Then look back over your life in this way and you might see it from a more positive perspective. You might see all the times you have been sent people to help you, to guide you and to look after you or challenge you.

I was probably about 17 the first time I read the following poem. It helped me to stop having intense focus on the 'why me?' feeling in my life and to see life as not just what was happening in my day right now but to put space between my feeling and my reaction. So instead of focusing on 'why me?' I could focus on the why. It opened up a whole new path for me and for the first time in my life to step back and see a different perspective – a bigger perspective.

FOOTPRINTS PRAYER

Footprints in the Sand

One night I had a dream ...
I dreamed I was walking along the beach with the Lord, and
Across the sky flashed scenes from my life.
For each scene I noticed two sets of footprints in the sand;
One belonged to me, and the other to the Lord.
When the last scene of my life flashed before us,
I looked back at the footprints in the sand.
I noticed that many times along the path of my life,
There was only one set of footprints.
I also noticed that it happened at the very lowest and saddest
    times in my life
This really bothered me, and I questioned the Lord about it.
"Lord, you said that once I decided to follow you,
You would walk with me all the way;
But I have noticed that during the most troublesome
    times in my life,
There is only one set of footprints.
I don't understand why in times when I needed you the most,
    you should leave me."
The Lord replied, "My precious, precious child. I love you,
    and I would never, never leave you during your times of
    trial and suffering.
When you saw only one set of footprints,
It was then that I carried you."

                                              Mary Stevenson

Life isn't about waiting for the storm to pass, it's about learning to dance in the rain.

— VIVIAN GREENE

EVERYTHING WE NEED

No life is a waste. The only time we actually waste is the time we spend thinking we are alone.

Everyone has a story to tell. Everyone's past – soul past, genetic past and personal past, has brought them to this point. Everyone can embrace where they have come from in order to understand where they are going. We get hints from our bodies, our souls and what happens around us every day. We have just stopped listening.

The universe will always provide for us what we need. When I was a teenager my mum wasn't around very much. I spent a lot of time miserable, wishing I had a mum like everyone else. Years later when I was looking back I wrote a list of all the things a 'MUM', in my eyes, would do – it was a big list but I can imagine you all have your own. Anyway, upon reflecting on this I realised that I had been given a mum all along – it just wasn't in the one person. My lack of seeing this had led me to always feel I hadn't had a proper mum. It was only when I looked at each thing, or the energy of a mum, that I could work it out.

You see between my nan, my sister, my brothers, my dad, a few teachers, a few neighbours, sport coaches, and a few girlfriends' mums, I actually had the best mum of all! My mum had so many life experiences to call on because she came from about 15 people. I had just never seen it that way or allowed myself to feel this. We will always be provided with what we need. Sometimes we just can't see it because it's not the way we want it. It's all in our perspective. And the way we want it would probably teach us nothing.

PASSPORT STAMPS

In discussions with these clients we have used the analogy of passport stamps, pieces of glitter, stepping stones stickers anything that means something to you can work.

I see many clients that work with troubled kids. From teachers, teachers' aides to police, psychologists, social workers, councillors and child-care workers.

Many of my clients have said more than once that they would like to take a child home and look after them. Often the people who work with children can be very upset becuase of what happens to them. So we discuss the bigger picture.

Let's look at this from a soul perspective. Each of these children is on a soul journey, that is they have come to Earth with a purpose, with something they want to learn. Often people start this journey very early on in life. So children can experience some very traumatic times. If we step back without our emotion for a second we can look at what that child feels: unloved, uncared for, abandoned, unimportant, unwelcome, powerless, etc.

You can then get an idea of what they are trying to learn which is the exact opposite of these feelings: loved, cared about, included, important, welcomed, empowered, etc.

The fact that you are in their life is because you remind them that they can feel all of these positive emotions …

Your presence in their life by just being you and by being in their life for even a short time is so important. You get to remind their soul what the positive feeling feels like to show them they are loveable, cared about, included, important, welcomed, etc., for who they are, because that is what they are here to learn. That is how it works: you are like a stamp in their life passport which they can always look back on, and a reminder to their soul to keep going. They need to have moments of the positive feeling during their journey to help them keep going. If we took on responsibility for them and took them home, took their pain away and made it all better we wouldn't be helping them achieve what they set out to achieve. We need to trust in their souls. Be grateful that you can be such a positive part of their soul journey as your lives cross paths.

Pain is temporary. It may last a minute, or an hour, or a day, or a year, but eventually it will subside. And something else will take its place. If I quit, however, it lasts forever.

LANCE ARMSTRONG

EMBRACE FEELINGS

N.B.: I have been asked more than once if it wise to use a quote from a drug cheat and a liar? My answer – of course Lance Armstrong may be a drug cheat and a liar, but he is also a soul just like you and I who is trying to learn all kinds of lessons. My ladder is sideways, and the quote is great!

Embrace feelings – they teach us about ourselves.

From a very young age we are taught not to feel, to suppress feelings and/or ignore them. We do anything we can to avoid them. Why do people eat a tub of ice-cream when they break up with partners? Well, when you were little and fell over someone gave you a lolly or a biscuit to distract you from the pain. Don't feel it, eat it!

When you needed your mum's attention and she was on the phone, instead of listening to why you and your brother were fighting, she gave you biscuits. Don't express it, eat it! Guess what! We formed a pattern.

It's like when the tuck-shop basket came into class and some people received lunch orders. We associated that with their being loved and special, that bad food is a treat. When you had lunch with your nanna and you had to eat your sandwich before you could have cake, we called cake a treat.

When you had to eat all your veggies before you could have sweets, sweets was a treat, a reward for you. BUT it is now somewhere in our pattern that junk food gives us the feeling of being loved and special so we treat ourselves with bad food. I see lots of clients trying to lose weight. Their feeling of being deprived and unloved while dieting comes up a lot. As well as working on the reasons why they have this in their life we also work on what is a treat. In our belief systems, high fat, sugary foods seem to be on most people's treat lists. So I want you to really think about how you feel when you eat McDonald's, after you eat creamy foods or anything else you think is a treat. Now think again. I don't want you to think emotionally this time I want you to remember how your body feels. Do you feel bloated, do you get diarrhoea, does your body want to sleep, do you have energy? How is that a treat for our bodies? Change what the word treat means.

Treat now means something that takes us more than two minutes to prepare. Imagine cutting up fresh fruit. Imagine the smell. You can even add yoghurt or muesli. Imagine how good your body feels after eating it. Imagine putting frozen strawberries in the blender with a banana and orange juice. Imagine making yourself the yummiest healthy sandwich. We associate treats with feeling loved. Remember to feel that, to acknowledge how much you love yourself and your body when you have your next treat.

CLIENT EXAMPLE
One of my clients, Mandy, couldn't stop buying clothes. She had a massive credit card debt and could spend nearly all of her wage on clothes each week. So we talked about this

for a while and what her feelings were around this and then we did a balance. She informed me that the only time she could stop buying clothes was when she was saving for an overseas trip. In fact she had done this a few times. Mandy was the youngest of four children and her parents had had her in their forties. When she was a little girl she was actually like an only child because her siblings had moved out, so she often felt alone. When they came to visit her they would always bring her something, a dress, shoes, hair ribbons. When she went out with them they would always buy her something. Her mum would often take her shopping. Mandy had developed a belief system that when she felt unloved and needed to feel special the fastest way for her to feel loved and special was to go and buy something. If she had had a hard day at work, or her partner was coming home late or her friend upset her, she would react by shopping. She had just never associated feeling like she was loved and special with her buying clothes!

When she was saving to go overseas she felt loved and special because she was doing something for herself. Saving for a holiday filled the gap of needing to feel loved and special so she didn't need to shop. We then worked on this belief system that she had created when she was younger. We also worked on some strategies that she could put into her life. Some ways and ideas she could use in her everyday life to ensure she continued to feel special and loved. You see we can't change that need in her because it's just part of her, so we embrace it. We understand it. Then she can smile at herself if she finds herself in a shop after a hard day at work and now instead of having no choice and no control over the situation she can choose. Buy the shoes or use one of her strategies! She now understands herself that much better.

FEELINGS OF GRIEF

Have you ever been to the funeral of a friend's aunt or similar, someone you have met only once? You go just to support your friend but you end up sobbing, feeling ridiculous and like you have no right to cry. It's because we link back the emotion to all the times we have felt grief for whatever reason and instead of feeling the moment at the time, we buried it and now feel it right back to the first time we experienced grief plus all the other times along the way. It's like a huge wave!

PERSONAL EXAMPLE

When my daughter passed away I learnt how inadequate we are in dealing with death. Some people will just walk away from your life because they can't deal with how they would feel, while other people can surprise you by being there when you least expect it.

Anyone who has experienced someone close to them dying can vouch for this. We want people to feel better, because we want to avoid feeling this pain, we use words to try to help. Words like, "At least you have other children", or "It's lucky she died this way maybe she would have been abducted otherwise", or "You are so strong. If it were me I would have killed myself by now". I promise these were words that really were said to me! Words like this can come out of our mouths because we feel inadequate and can't make it better. Sometimes you just can't make things better.

The best response I got was from my dad. He said to me, "Come here, I will just hug you while you cry!" Tears are not scary, they are a wonderful way really to feel an emotion and move through it. When anyone in my life dies now I will no longer be afraid. I want to feel it, to embrace it, to own that feeling, because I have loved that person – I don't want to just make it go away. Things in life can hurt. When my child died it felt like I had been ripped in two and it was for me the worst emotional pain I have ever felt in my life. However, since I allowed myself to feel it, I am no longer afraid, because of this, I am thankful because now I am free and I am able to love so much better.

Many people were surprised that my husband or I didn't take anti-depressant tablets. We are so scared as a society to feel and emotionally respond to life that it is now more normal than not to turn to tablets to help us suppress our feelings. This is because all our pain is like stacks on, like a Lego tower that we have been building our whole life. No one ever teaches us to embrace it. In fact the thought of feeling the emotion can sometimes be scarier than actually embracing and moving through that emotion.

The fact is that death is the guarantee in life and we will all experience grief for loved ones we have lost, yet we don't embrace it at all.

It is interesting to note that everyone I have talked to who has lost a child rarely ask each other how, because it doesn't really matter, but everyone else will ask how. I have often wondered why this is the case and I have come up with two things. Firstly, because they want to understand the story to see how they might feel if it were them; and secondly, because they want to see if that could happen to them, if they could control the situation.

You see, every question has a feeling behind it. Every question is really about us and trying to work out things in ourselves. Every answer invokes a feeling in the other person. Feelings would be different if I said I left the pool gate open and she drowned, or she wandered out the front and was hit by a car, or I left her for five minutes to get milk and the house burnt down, compared to lightning striking her, or her dying in her sleep. We all feel something different with each of these different responses. We are trying to work out whose fault it is, not to blame the person who lost their child but to see if it could happen to us or if we could avoid it happening. The different feelings we get from "I left the pool gate open", or "She was struck by lightning", lead us to think we can control the pool gate, or not allow our child to go out in a storm. A perfect example of this is if I said she was killed in a car accident, the next question would always be what happened. The person isn't really asking what happened, they are asking whose fault it was, because they are trying to work out their feeling, their response and if they could control the situation.

CHILDHOOD HINTS

If we go back to our childhood and instead of reliving traumatic experiences we can look at positive things to help us understand ourselves. What was your favourite storybook? In going through the story that was your favourite it is because somehow you identified with this. It may be the character, the time, the location or the story itself. If we understand it, it will really be the feeling it gave you that is the most important thing. This can give you an insight into what your soul was looking for even as a child. I have done this at times with lots of clients and the significance that story plays in their life today is amazing. Fascinating really, just another hint that we get to understand ourselves.

Every response, every feeling you have to everything, every second of the day, is actually about you, an insight into yourself. Unfortunately, we are taught from a very young age not to listen but to project our feelings onto others. It's really just a way to avoid ourselves. It is about you, who you are, where you came from and who you want to be.

Feelings are just secret hints we get to help us understand ourselves. Don't be afraid to feel, it frees the soul.

You must be the change you wish to see in the world.

GANDHI

ANGER

Anger is my favourite emotion. We are taught from a young age that we need to deal with our anger – which means *don't show it, suppress it*.

We do the same thing with anger as we do with grief. We hold it in and we let it build up and up and up. It really is like a volcano and the next minute we lose it because someone pulled out in front of us or someone bumped us or knocked over the milk. We are not dealing with the anger from that moment, we are riding a wave of anger that we have been sitting on – kind of like a volcano that blows! We need to embrace our emotions at the time and feel them and move through them and not be scared to do this.

When anger is really intense it is sometimes hard to work through it. Being active, running, going for a walk, listening to music, going outside and screaming at the top of your lungs, punching a pillow or punching bag, drawing, scribbling, tearing up pieces of paper are all wonderful ways to deintensify the anger feeling. However, what happens is we do this but we don't actually embrace the anger and understand it. We do this to release it but if we don't work it out it will build up again and then we have a continuous cycle that is actually a block in our life.

Real anger is a wonderful thing because when you have it, it can change your life and change the world. If you were angry about the way you were taught as a child you may actually become a teacher. Perhaps you didn't get picked for the team you wanted so now you work twice as hard. Angry people are very empowered people.

My daughter said to me the other day that rejection, which is in the anger family, can be a wonderful thing, it makes you not take things for granted and it makes you work harder.

WORKING ANGER OUT

When people are angry they can unknowingly provoke people to make them be angry at them too.

For example, you are struggling to get your life together, whether it be school, home or work. You feel really disempowered and blame everyone else: "It's my boss, he's an arse" or "The teachers can't explain stuff" or "My partner keeps nagging me".

You then come home with attitude, you snap at everyone around you, you feel like a victim and think everyone hates you.

What is really happening is that deep down you are angry at yourself, so angry that you try your best to piss everyone off and make them angry at you too.

This you are really good at!

Now everyone is on your case, so this justifies why you can't achieve anything, because everyone and everything is against you. You have no luck in life.

Sound familiar?

So what is your soul saying? That's where you have to become creative. Sure you are angry but what's underneath that? Frustration? Can't please everyone? What does your soul want? What's under that?

"I don't know what I want to do." (Stop comparing yourself to other people.) I feel helplessness – what's under that?

Underneath all this anger is disempowerment. I have dropped all my power on the floor, or given it all away. I don't want responsibility. Life scares me! What's under that?

Why, because I don't trust.

Okay, so now tell me why you don't trust.

What experiences have you been through that lead you to here?

What is under that?

I don't feel safe.

Okay, so now you really understand yourself and can look at not feeling safe and how you can empower yourself to feel safe and to trust again. What you can add into your life helps you do this.

When we stop being angry at everyone and work out that we are really angry at ourselves we can embrace that kind of anger. We now have the opportunity to make great changes in our lives. It is so wonderful to see someone work this out.

We don't see things as they are,

we see things as we are.

ANAIS NIN

EVERYTHING IS A MIRROR

Every feeling you have is all about you.

If a person is angry at you, it is because they are angry at themselves because they can't fix it.

If a person is reacting to a situation there are emotions all over it. But the real emotion they are feeling is about them, they just can't see it. For example, if someone is angry at a person for not helping with something like a school fete, they might just be angry at themselves because they can't say 'No!'

If you are angry at a partner because they just sit by the clothes that need folding and watch TV, it's because you are angry at yourself because you won't allow yourself to stop and do something for yourself.

If you are angry that someone left your workplace, you may really be upset and feel inadequate with yourself because you wanted to help them more and you feel you didn't get the chance. Every reaction to something, every feeling we have about something is really hiding a feeling we have about ourselves. You can't have the other person's feeling because you are not them – you are *you* and the feeling you have is all about *you*.

Feelings are the language of the soul. Your soul wants you

to feel it, work out what it is and really feel it. If it means you cry, then cry, or punch a punching bag, or write. But embrace the feeling, work it out, don't focus on other people and blame, don't run away from it and don't hide from it, *own it*. You can't be a victim this way, you can only be responsible for you. We need to embrace Earth emotions and work through them.

FEEL IT ... UNDERSTAND IT ... OWN IT ... MOVE IT.

Sometimes it can't be made better. Sometimes we just need to cry without anyone trying to make it better, to release the overwhelming feeling, not to be scared by how intense an emotion can feel. If we feel it, it will dissipate and move. We can spend so long avoiding feeling it, that sometimes the fear of feeling it is worse and lasts longer than the feeling itself!

Identify your key feeling underneath.

Fear, Trust, Scared, Safe, Free, etc.

Understand where that fits into your life and then work out ways that will help you embrace this, so trying to avoid that feeling no longer has control over your life.

Put it back to, "If I was the only person ever in my space would I still feel this? Is it because I am comparing myself to others, to what they would think? Am I stopping my soul from being me?"

Once you do this, things have no choice but to move on because you have finished that lesson. Your soul is ready for the next one. It won't wait because that is why we are here.

Stop being afraid of what could go wrong and start being positive about what could go right.

UNKNOWN

Don't waste your time looking

back on what you've lost.

Move on, for life is not meant

to be travelled backwards.

UNKNOWN

CLEARING FEELINGS

Sometimes life experiences are really meant to be experienced only once. What I mean is that some of our experiences are so traumatic that we shut the box never to be opened again. For some people counselling can be very traumatic because at times it means you have to re-live everything that happened. I don't think we should have to re-live things, ever, especially when they are that bad. Those situations really just take our power away and reinforce the feeling of being helpless or a victim.

However, I am aware that every experience is a life lesson, so sometimes we need to diminish the intensity of the situation and the emotions before we can look at what it is we felt so that we can understand what it is we are trying to learn. Through kinesiology I learnt some wonderful ways to minimise the intensity of emotions. I put together a program some years ago which I ran for primary schools. It is not just for primary school children but can be used by anybody at any age. It is very simple and can be used for intense situations or even daily, like a quick cleanse before bed! It is designed to help minimise intense feelings that stop us from being the person we want to be, and our soul wants us to be.

Think of a situation:

1. **Feel your feeling.** (Normally a yuck feeling.)
   Identify what your feeling is:

Are you	Angry	Unhappy
	Sad	Confused
	Scared	Alone
	Worried	Or something else?

2. **Find where it is in your body.**
   Ask yourself does it make you want to run, to curl up in a ball, punch something ...
   Can you feel it in your:
   Hands   Head   Legs   Chest or anywhere else?

3. **Give your feeling a colour.**
   Any colour you give your feeling is okay. It's your feeling, so your colour is always right.
   Is it thick, thin, heavy, light, hot, cold, hard, soft?

4. **Get rid of your yucky feeling.**
   Take five to ten deep breaths. As you breathe out blow your colour out along with your yuck feeling. Make sure there is no feeling or colour left.

5. **Remember a time when you felt wonderful.**
   Examples: Nice and safe – maybe in bed all snuggled up.
   A time you felt really proud of yourself.
   A time when everything went right.

6. **Give that good feeling a colour.**
   Any colour you give your feeling is okay. It's your feeling so your colour is always right.

7. **Breathe in that wonderful colour.**
   Make sure you can feel it:
   All the way down to your toes.
   Let it fill up your legs.
   Your chest and arms and back.
   Your neck, shoulders and head.
   Wrap the colour around you.

8. When you are finished take a moment to experience how wonderful you feel.

9. Remember, any time you experience a feeling that is too intense to embrace, you can do this.

For example, if you are having a bad day, just stop and breathe out the yuck feeling in five big breaths. Then take five big breaths of the colour that made you feel safe, or proud of yourself. Now see how much better you feel!

Often with a balance clearing the intensity of feelings like this can then help us clear things on a much deeper level resulting in a much better understanding the client then has of themselves.

When you find yourself cocooned in isolation and despair and cannot find your way out of the darkness, remember that this is similar to the place where caterpillars go to grow their wings!

UNKNOWN

BREAKDOWNS

Breakdowns happen when we stop listening altogether. The name says it all – BREAKDOWN. It means we need to BREAK – IT – DOWN. Break down every aspect of our life, everything we are doing. We need to make things small again, focus on one thing at a time and do things one at a time. It's often because we have lost ourselves. We don't understand ourselves. We have avoided ourselves for too long. We have been so busy trying to keep everyone else happy that we can't feel or be anything close to who we are meant to be. One of my favourite quotes: *"Whilst thinking of others may superficially seem like kindness, it's actually a selfish technique to stop you thinking of yourself."* by Russell Brand.

How do we begin to find ourselves? Well the first thing is to get to know yourself.

Begin by writing a list.

Write a list of the things you like: going for a walk on a sunny day, laughing, Vegemite toast, family dinners, camping, listening to music and so on.

Add to the list for 24 hours, including everything you can think of, then leave the list for a day or two and make a time with yourself to go back to it. This gives your thoughts space and allows them to settle.

Sit down and look at each thing individually and ask yourself, "Do I really like this? Do I do it to keep everyone else happy?" Cross off anything on the list that you 'like' that you do for everyone else.

Here's the best bit. Everything on your list has a feeling associated with it. Go back through your list again and write the feeling that you get with each thing.

For example:

Going for a walk on a sunny day.	Freedom and peace.
Laughing.	Joy.
Vegemite toast.	Safe.
Family dinners.	Belonging.
Camping.	Freedom and peace.
Listening to music.	Awe, inspiration.

Now you start to see the feelings that you want in your life. This is you, so now we work on finding the things that give you any of these feelings. And then finding new things you can try or add that give you this feeling like finding a job, finding a sport, or a group of like-minded people. Now you are beginning to know who you are.

Imagine if you had that peace-filled feeling every day! It really is meant to be like heaven on Earth here. We really can have that.

Most people have holidays on their list. In fact so many people trudge through their year just hanging out for that two weeks when they can take their holiday to wherever. It's not the holiday we want it's the feeling we get on holiday –

the peace, no guilt, no trying to keep everyone else happy. We don't have to be anything to anyone when we are on holiday! Find ways to bring and acknowledge that holiday feeling into your everyday life, even if it's just for five minutes, i.e. have a quick bath, or look at the stars as you walk in the door, put music on, ring someone because you want to, sit outside while you have a cup of tea in the evening or coffee in the morning, anything that helps you have that feeling. Most people on holidays don't watch TV. Turn off the TV, it can add hours back into your life that have been disappearing and making your life feel way too busy. We love TV so much because we can get lost in someone else's world and not have to live in our own.

Turn 'have tos' into 'choose tos'. So many people say I have to … and then begrudgingly go along and complete their 'have to' all the while being grumpy, resentful and drained of energy. Be aware there are no 'have tos' in life. You could have said NO – I am aware that there are consequences however if we deal with facts there is a choice. So next time you think you 'have to' 'flip it', that is turn over, turn it into a 'choose to'. It's a state of mind, when we 'choose to' and we embrace doing something it gives us energy. It becomes something positive in our life.

Incorporate all of this into your life every day. This is how life is meant to feel. We need to bring peace and peaceful empowerment into our everyday life, especially that holiday feeling. We need to be able to keep our peace (holiday!) at all times regardless of what is going on around us.

LIKE YOURSELF

Now that you are beginning to know yourself it's time to like yourself.

By working on what you like, you now understand how you want to feel. You know yourself that little bit better. Those feelings that you discovered about yourself are facts. They can't be changed, they are simply facts. No different from the sky is blue or the grass is green, or the sun is hot.

In fact when we start to really discover who we are, the truth is facts.

So you might be a person who is a safe, with life themes of rejection and abandonment. You like feeling connected, important, and responsible. You would love to own a business but you are scared. Meeting new people can be challenging.

Awesome. None of this is changeable they are just facts. So we no longer need to apologise to anyone for who we are. No longer do we have to wait for anyone else's opinion to like us, no longer do we need to make excuses for ourselves and no longer do we need to block ourselves because we know us, we are who we are!

We can now put in place achievable goals, things we can work towards. We can help other people help us because we understand us, we know what we need and now we can ask.

ASKING FOR HELP

We grow up in a world that asking for help is seen as a weakness. We avoid asking for help at all costs and when we finally have no choice due to circumstances and have to ask for help we reluctantly ask for help yet all we can feel is guilt. Let's turn this around. Asking for help empowers people, it gives them a feeling of purpose. We all like helping people yet we all take that privilege away from other people. Change it, ask for help when necessary and enjoy the feeling of helping and purpose that you allowed others the opportunity to have! Like the fact that we are all in this together.

DATE YOURSELF

I love this idea. This is homework I set for many of my clients. It reminds them how to begin to really enjoy who they are and to get to know themselves. It is particularly good when you have broken up from a relationship, however, it is fun and worthwhile to do anytime.

How do you date yourself? If you were planning to take someone out for a night, or to help someone feel loved and looked after, then you would plan lots of surprises for them. You may send them phone messages, make a wonderful dinner, book them in for a massage, take them on a walk on a beach or in a park, you may run a bath for them, you may dress up for them. So many things that you have probably already done to make someone else's day special.

Do this: send yourself a text message, write yourself a letter and post it, spend some time making beautiful healthy meals, take yourself to the movies, or a walk, rub moisturiser into your skin. Smile at yourself in the mirror, pick yourself flowers, play billards against yourself, float in a pool. Even do things like clean out your car or when you clean your house enjoy it, do it for you because you love it clean.

Date yourself for a day, a week, a month, a year, better

still, for the rest of your life! It is so much fun. You really are the only person who knows exactly how you like things.

The feeling of being in love comes from feeling so special when there is someone else that wants to do all these things for us. Why then can't we be 'in love' with ourselves. Try it and see just how good your day is!

Believe in yourself and all that you are, know that there is something inside you that is greater than any obstacle.

CHRISTIAN D LARSON

You are responsible for how you feel no matter what someone does to you. Remember, you are always in control of your thoughts so choose to feel confident and adequate rather than angry and insecure.

WWW.LIVELIFEHAPPY.COM

BAKE YOUR CAKE!

My favourite little 'story'!

I use this example a lot with clients and the look on their face when they get it is just beautiful. However, on occasion I have had to change the analogy, especially when dealing with male clients, so we have painted a car, designed tattoos, built a man cave! Please feel free to insert the appropriate task that works for you.

I am going to a dinner party and I want to bring something, so I spend all day making a cake. It's not just any cake but a magnificent chocolate and black cherry cake, beautifully decorated. It looks amazing. I bring this cake and put it in the middle of the table for everyone to share. As the night goes on no one comments. I cut the cake and no one takes a piece. In fact, nothing is said and after everyone has left, the cake still remains in the middle of the table. How should I feel? … Shattered, hurt, or upset are the most common responses I get.

You see we wait until everyone says, "OMG this cake is amazing!" or "it tastes so good!" or "it looks perfect!" etc. That's when we feel good about our cake (or really ourselves).

We wait. We bring who we are forward and then we wait

for someone to tell us they like us, that we are okay. We give ourselves permission to like ourselves, but it's based on what they think, they hold all our power!

The fact is, I like baking cakes so I need to like myself when I bake the cake (or sew the quilt, or coach the footy team, or put in the proposal I did for work). We need to like ourselves by doing what we do, not when people tell us *they* like what we do.

This is relevant to every aspect of our lives, especially if we are in charge of or overseeing something. Here's the secret – like yourself while you bake your cake!

Often we can block ourselves from doing things because we don't think we are good enough. So we don't rebuild a car, or tackle that craft project, or try that home renovation. We only do things we know people will tell us we are amazing at, because that is the only way we have to feel good about ourselves, when the end result is fantastic. This limits us from trying, learning and experiencing all aspects of life. Feel good about yourself because you are you, before you start anything, and while you are doing it even if it turns out to be a disaster you allowed yourself the learning journey. We are not meant to be perfect at everything.

My kids have taken this story to school, to share with their friends. 'Bake your Cake' has become a phrase their friends say to each other to remind them to not lose focus of feeling good about themselves. I love this!

No man can succeed in a line of endeavor which he does not like.

NAPOLEON HILL

Part 6

UNDERSTANDING OUR RELATIONSHIPS ON EARTH

You must learn a new way

to think before you can

master a new way to be.

MARIANNE WILLIAMSON

UNDERSTANDING OUR REACTIONS TO PEOPLE

Be careful not to put people on pedestals, you will only be disappointed. Being on a pedestal allows that person not to have any life lessons, not to be able to make mistakes. They, and you, will end up disillusioned. Putting people on pedestals means that your ladder can never be turned sideways. Instead of putting people on pedestals allow yourself to admire them. Find what it is you like in them, what quality is it – it could be their determination, their ability to focus, the way they cope with life. The reason we are attracted to each other in this way is because the quality you like in that person is the quality in you that your soul is working on. I promise you that the same thing you like in them is in you! You just need to wake it up! Allow yourself to be inspired by them. They are a hint in your life to help you understand yourself and to give you a hint on who you are meant to be.

When you meet someone you admire or someone you hate this is not a coincidence.

When you meet someone you hate, it really isn't the other person you hate it is your recognition or sense of that same type of self in you or someone from your past that has left you with feelings you haven't dealt with – an untouched opportunity to understand yourself. Part of you is looking in a mirror, and you need to look at why you don't like them to help you discover what it is in you that you need to look at. If you didn't need to look at it, it wouldn't get to you! Ask yourself, "Does this person remind me of me or something about me?" Or what is it they are doing that I don't like? Is it, for example, laziness, arrogance or avoidance. Be honest with yourself.

The other reason you may meet someone you hate is because it is giving you an opportunity to clear something from your past. Ask yourself, "Who in my past does this person remind me of?" Sometimes it's really hard to work out so don't think of looks, think of temperament, of what it is they are implying or doing and *how do I feel* around them. Is that the same feeling I got around mum or dad or a teacher, or any other person in my life?

Clients I work with are quite surprised when we do a balance and they discover the woman at work who annoys them so much is giving them the same feeling their sister did when they were nine. Or they realise they keep yelling at their daughter because she represents their own mum. It's really fascinating but it also shows how we repeat feelings, and repeat how we react to situations time and time again until we deal with the why behind it.

I don't want you to save me,

I want you to stand by my side

while I save myself.

UNKNOWN

At any given moment you have the power to say: this is not how the story is going to end.

UNKNOWN

THE REAL STORY

Are there things in your life you don't like? If you had a magic wand what would you change?

This is a question I ask nearly every client. If I gave you a magic wand what would you change? I ask this because I get a hint about what is not working for them. However, I focus on the feeling underneath it and what that means not the situation they are describing.

It's fantastic to know what we want to change but most people just want it to go away. We can't really change it unless we understand it, unless we work out how we got here in the first place. If we just make it go away, then we will find ourselves in a similar situation in the near future.

The following can be the same in any relationship, with our partners, our parents, our kids or our friends.

Let's take a marriage for example. So many women and men I see feel trapped, unloved and unappreciated, but they have created this. Over the years they have allowed each other to behave in certain ways. They have developed a list of unwritten rules so to speak! They never communicate how they really feel. They never look at themselves and they always blame the other person. If they do try to communicate, most sentences have the word *you* in it: when you, you don't, you always. They aren't looking at how they really feel about what is going on. They never think they have to change, they think their partner needs to change.

If you are unhappy in your relationship then … **Take responsibility! You created this!**

TUG OF WAR LOVE

Once upon a time two people met and began a relationship. Both people were desperate to look after each other, in fact, when they looked after the other person they each felt really good about themselves. They both had lots of love and energy to bring into the relationship. So much so that they got such a kick out of seeing the other person happy that they stopped loving themselves, and just focused on loving the other person. They didn't need to love themselves as much anymore because the other person was just so good at it. Everything the other person did made them feel happy.

Many years later both people find themselves in a relationship where they are exhausted, unappreciated, feel unloved, disconnected and they can't work out what happened. So what really happened? Both people underneath are trying to say, "I am so exhausted because I spend all day trying to make you happy and nothing I do is good enough anymore, it doesn't work anymore. I am so exhausted because I am empty I have no love coming in and I so don't know how to love myself anymore. I rely on you to love me for me because I can't love myself, you used to do that and now that doesn't happen anymore." Now we try to drag love from each other.

Even daily tasks become a competition such as:

"How was work?"

"Exhausting. I am so tired."

"You're so tired? OMG I have spent all day running the kids around, parent-teacher interviews, sport, etc. At least you went to bed last night at 9.00 p.m. I didn't get to bed until 2.00 a.m. after making the lunches."

Response: "Well at least you can get up at 7.30 a.m., I have to get up at 5.00 a.m.

WATER YOUR OWN GARDEN
(my other favourite story)

Imagine all of us have a watering can. I spend my day using my watering can to fill other people's watering cans so that they can water their own gardens. I fill my children's watering cans with the care I give them each day. I fill the watering cans of my friends, my husband, the school, my parents, my work colleagues, my clients, my staff, etc. I fill other people's watering cans all day long. As I go to bed I top up my family's watering cans to make sure they are full for the morning. Then I go to bed and one day I wake up and my can is empty so I am angry at my husband and my family. I feel unappreciated, uncared for and unloved. Our mothers, fathers or carers used to fill watering cans before we got married and had our family, I always woke up with a full watering can every morning. Now it's empty I am especially angry at my husband. Why is my can empty? It's not fair!

Whose responsibility is it to fill my watering can?

MINE and only MINE.

Past generations taught us to do for others and sacrifice ourselves. If my watering can is empty I can't help anyone. I should never *expect* anyone else to fill mine. I am the only one responsible for me, I need to fill mine. I can receive a bonus by having someone else top mine up but I must always make sure mine is not empty.

We need to teach our families, our spouses and our children to fill their own watering cans. I never want anyone I love to wake up with empty watering cans. I have to SHOW them how to fill their own by showing them how I fill mine, before I make sure theirs is full. I have to teach them that to take time for themselves is essential so that they can listen to what their own soul is saying. Then they can add water to whoever's watering can they want because I showed them how to fill their own by filling mine and now theirs will never empty.

EMBRACE CHANGING YOU

If we begin to love ourselves properly, to fill our own watering cans, to listen to what our bodies are telling us about ourselves, then competing for attention with our partner will change. Imagine if your partner came home and you said, "Hi beautiful, how are you?" To which they reply, "Exhausted. How are you? I imagine you are exhausted you had a really big week. You should do something really nice for yourself this weekend, you deserve it. I think I'll do something nice for myself too. I think I'll add some bath time to my schedule this weekend." You see, by loving yourself you teach them that they should love themselves too. You can't change people, you can only inspire them to change themselves, and you do this by being you! Stop competing. Stop trying to make them love you and love yourself instead – it rubs off.

Stay married to them but date yourself. Let them stay married to you but let them date themselves. After all you both know exactly what you need.

So many of my client's focus on the other person. Their magic wand moment is if their partner could change. They want their partner to change, to stop or start doing something. They forget that the issue at hand is not what their partner does. The issue and what they are meant to look at is why they personally react to this situation in such a way. The lesson is understanding our reaction. When we do this, when we embrace this, it gives us the opportunity to communicate without manipulating.

Lessons are never one way, even though at times it is easy and yet frustrating to see the other person's lessons and their failure to learn and instead continually create the same situation for themselves over and over again.

We can often feel frustrated because that person might be our spouse or our child. We think we can't do anything and we feel resentful because we can't change it.

STOP!

You can never experience anything without there being a lesson in it for you. Work out what that is, why you respond the way you do. You can only change yourself. Your job is to understand yourself Then, by just being you, you can inspire someone else to change themselves!

Another reason why relationships fail is because we stay in the same space we were in when we met our partner.

PERSONAL EXAMPLE

When I first met Paul I put him on a pedestal. He was strong and he made me feel safe, looked after and believed in me. He believed in me so much that it rubbed off and I started to believe in myself. Things became harder for a while because I was unsure of how to be strong and independent, I didn't want to rock the boat, I wanted to avoid confrontation at all cost. We were both used to him making it better for me and I was scared to change that. When we started our family I stayed home and studied so it was easy for me to go back to him being the one who looked after us all. As the children grew older and our last baby went to primary school things changed again. I had become so busy seeing clients at home that I needed to move my business elsewhere, so I bought a local business where I could see my clients. However, I was aware that I didn't want him to feel not needed so I changed myself. I also hated confrontation so I would never say how I felt, I would just stew on the inside. I would be different at home to what I was at work. Then one day I realised something about myself. I had been married to my husband for about 16 years. I would go to work, see clients and talk to them about things. I would say how I felt, no matter how confronting that was for the other person. I was the person I believed I was meant to be. Then at home I realised I wasn't doing this. I wasn't allowing myself to be me. So I had a good long think.

I wanted to change the rules that I had made at home. I was changing all the situations I had created and had allowed to happen. Instead of blaming him and wanting him to change, **I** had to change. Instead of me being angry at him (because it's a mirror it really meant I was angry with myself and what I had created) I spoke to him about my journey, about what I had discovered about myself, how I wasn't happy with not being me all the time at home, of how I was scared of confrontation so I wouldn't say how I felt, and I embraced my lesson.

We had spoken about it and we were both on the same page. He was aware of exactly what I was working on for myself personally. I allowed myself to say how I really felt. We talked about many things. After some time together it took a while to work out what the base feeling actually was, but it was such an empowering situation for us both. I never wanted a new husband. However, I had to allow me to be me and not be scared to introduce my old husband to my real me! I had to let go of my feelings of needing to be safe so I could make sure he never left, because this was preventing me from really being me!

Those who cannot change their minds cannot change anything.

GEORGE BERNARD SHAW

COMMUNICATION

We don't communicate effectively at all! We try to communicate with each other without words. If you are upset or angry about something people can tell. What is wrong they ask? Nothing, you reply as you continue to sulk, or snap at people or throw things. It's pretty clear that something is wrong, but now they have to guess. That's not fun or effective for anyone.

When we do try to communicate with our words we turn them around to try to change the other person without taking any responsibility for ourselves or using the situation as an opportunity to embrace, understand and move on from something we are meant to learn for ourselves.

We say things like: you make me feel inadequate, you make me feel stupid, you make me feel so unappreciated, you make me feel so unloved. Or we become clever and say when you fall asleep in front of the TV, I feel abandoned, when you talk on the phone all night to your girlfriend, I feel like you don't care about me.

Remember NO ONE CAN MAKE YOU FEEL. A feeling is a feeling, it's your feeling, your secret way to understand yourself. OWN IT. Don't blame someone else for your feeling. You cannot feel inadequate unless you already feel inadequate – your feeling of inadequacy was already there before they did anything. If you try to turn it around by saying "When you …", you just made them responsible to fix things for you. How exhausting for them when they don't know how to make you truly happy when it is not now or ever supposed to be their job, it's your job.

PERSONAL EXAMPLE

I remember a very long time ago I was putting the plates away (rather loudly), feeling very angry and unappreciated while my husband was in the lounge room. I was trying to get his attention. "He could at least put the dishes away," I thought. He came in and I tried to rip his head off! He casually replied, "Honey I don't see the dishes, I am not designed like that, but if you ask me I will gladly help!" Don't ever assume other people know how you feel, and don't use actions to tell them, use your words. It's much quicker and more empowering for both of you.

Words really are hidden secret messages to how a soul feels. The thing to work out in an argument is what is it that I am really feeling? You see, I was angry that my husband did not see the dishes, or could watch TV lying by the clothes that need to be folded! I really wasn't angry at him – I was trying to make him feel sorry for me because I had to do it (I had to do the dishes because my list of Earth rules at that time said I have to have everything done before I can sit down!) Really what I get angry about is the fact that I can't sit down when things are messy and do nothing, or relax. Really I am angry at me – the fact that I don't allow myself to relax, or say what I need. That was my issue in this. That is what I had to work on!

So let's break this down further. When I understand myself, I know that I can't sit down while things are messy. So now I get a choice. I can ask for help and normally people do help, however if no one helps I can now choose my reaction. Instead of the dishes or washing being a 'have to' I can turn it into a 'choose to'. I can embrace it and enjoy it because I want it done for me. Really I am doing it to make me feel better. Or I can choose to do it later and be okay with that. The whole situation is about me and what I want and finding the best outcome for me. I was trying to manipulate other people to do things for me, especially by having a tantrum. Now that I understand myself I can communicate my truth. "I find it hard to relax unless my house is clean." As a family we can all work on that. That doesn't mean that my husband and kids will keep the house perfectly clean. It does mean they understand the bigger picture – my picture. They know if I am having a tantrum to get what I want that it is about me. It means when it comes to people visiting or days I want a clean house we can communicate better and work together because they understand where I am really coming from. It also means they can help me embrace leaving things out of place from time to time.

CLIENT EXAMPLE

I had a client who was so particular about things that her house was always spotless. Before she went to bed all the dishes were done, even the ironing was finished and away. These were her expectations she had adopted over the years.

She even colour matched the pegs when she put the clothes on the line. The problem with this was that her expectations were unmovable, which means it really created a stress for her if we talked about changing any of her routine. We did a balance around her expectations and belief systems these related to. Her homework over the next few weeks was to be able to leave a dirty cup on the sink, smile at herself, and go to bed. She also had to close her eyes when she pulled the pegs from the basket. Now her expectations are movable and she is free to choose. She can embrace the way she works but if there are days she can't do it all it doesn't create any stress, she can just smile at herself.

PAINT A PICTURE

Sometimes understanding words can be really difficult. A great way to help yourself or someone else find where they are emotionally or to help someone else feel where you are at, is to paint a picture with your words.

If I say to you, "I feel alone", you can only go to a time where you felt alone to identify with this.

However if I say to you, "I feel like I am in a well. It's cold and it's dark. I have been treading water for eight hours and I am exhausted. I can't see the entrance to the well because it is bent," you now see and can feel exactly where I am at.

Or if I say, "I am in a battlefield, surrounded by rubble as far as the eye can see. There is no one else around and I have no idea which way to go," you understand exactly where I am, exactly what my 'alone' is right now.

You can and need to create a picture that makes how you feel, or someone else feels, perfectly clear. This is really important when talking with other people, otherwise they will think that your 'alone' means their 'alone' or your 'overwhelmed' means their 'overwhelmed' because you have both had different life experiences. To understand you, they need to step into your storybook and word pictures are the perfect way to do that. It takes away their assumption from their life experience and allows them to feel what it is you are feeling. It works especially well with children to help them understand you and for you to understand them.

Life is really a journey of self-discovery, however, we are meant to have people help us along the way.

The tiny seed knew that in order to grow, it needed to be dropped in dirt, covered in darkness, and struggle to reach the light.

UNKNOWN

ROCK STORY

One of the most common lessons our souls learn is the rock story. So many clients have experienced this one way or another, whether it be with a partner, parent or other.

Imagine you have one rock sitting on top of another.

This is when two people meet. One is strong and the other is struggling with life, so the strong rock takes control. It sits on top of the other to protect it from harm. Eventually the rock underneath starts to feel strong again and wants to move next to the strong rock, but the rock won't let it. The top rock only feels good about itself when it protects. How can it feel good about itself if it can't protect? So it doesn't let the underneath rock out. It is scared that things will change, scared the underneath rock will no longer need it. The underneath rock is now squashed and can't breathe. The underneath rock will eventually fight, and fight hard to be free.

We need to break our rocks to find our seed!

Instead of being rocks, imagine we are seeds planted next to each other. Both are growing at different times and both are providing protection for each other by using their leaves to shelter the other. Both are flowering at different times. Both use each other's branches as support to help each other grow further. Both allow each other to grow in different directions at times whilst always having their roots grounded in the same place!

Are you a rock or a beautiful plant? Find what you need to change so you can be a beautiful plant.

Help others find their seed and plant them together. Don't be scared of each other or of change. Be in awe of each other and of the opportunity for change and what it can show and teach us.

In life one person is not meant to be on top of another, squashing them. We are meant to be next to each other. We will grow and understand our lessons at different times. In relationships, we are meant to be next to each other, to be the people we are meant to be. Only then can we help and inspire others to grow, just by being us.

People try to stop each other from changing. "I was happy at 22 when I met you. Be that person, don't change, I want you to do everything the same." They do this because they are scared to look at themselves. They remember at the start of the relationship they were happy so they just want everything to stay that way. The problem with that is life happens. We get opportunities to learn about ourselves every day. Life is like a river that flows, it continues to move, to change every single day. A river can't be stopped. Imagine being in a flowing river. Here you are in your boat, clinging to an overhanging tree branch for dear life, refusing to let go, trying to stop yourself from flowing down the river. It takes up so much more energy than sitting back in your boat and enjoying the ride. Sometimes people even appear to be trying to paddle upstream!

Not dealing with emotions, not feeling them, embracing them or moving them blocks the flow of life. You may be with a person and you have both learnt what you were meant to learn from each other, yet you cling on for dear life.

There are many ways that we block the flow of life. If you hold on to a job that makes you unhappy you block the person who is meant to do that job and be happy in it. If you don't move house you block the person who is meant to live in and love your house, if you don't let a relationship go you block the next people in both your lives from helping you with the next step, the next lessons for your soul.

Sometimes when you let go of something that was once special to you, you are not really losing it you are passing it on to someone else.

The only thing you are meant to do in a relationship is BE YOU – the **soul** you.

What if you are the squashed rock? How do you change that? Do you just leave? Remember there is always a lesson in it for you and you will repeat it if you don't embrace it. Firstly, you allowed yourself to be squashed! Secondly, the person who is squashing you feels safe there. So not only are you changing but (GUILT FREE!) you are giving them the opportunity to change, a creative learning opportunity.

Too often people just leave relationships without looking at themselves and what they have created. You need to change yourself, not the other person, but you need to do it gently and with love and communication and when they react, you need to hear what their soul is saying not the words they are using. Change appears scary but really it is freeing.

You can't change another person. Many people stay in a relationship because they can see the potential of the other person. They put all their energy into trying to make them realise that potential. They nag and they suggest what the other person should do. They might even send off resumes for them or book them into courses.

People will change by themselves, however, no one can change in an environment where they feel unworthy, unloved, unsupported and manipulated.

The only thing you can do is create an environment where people feel safe and secure and then they have the opportunity to change. They may not, but you gave them all the love and support you could and you worked out what your lesson was by attracting this situation into your life. Once you embrace and learn your lesson things may change. It certainly will within you. I can't promise you the other person will change, that is up to them, if they haven't learnt what they were meant to learn from this life experience then they will repeat the lesson with someone else or in some other way in their life.

I am not saying we need to treat relationships lightly and move on continuously. What I am saying is about you. You need to be *you*, you need to find your peace, to love yourself, to date yourself and to know and understand yourself. Then you can be happy and feel free and not be what or who you think the other person wants you to be. You don't find this by leaving and then repeating the lesson you were trying to learn. Learn it first. Change things now and challenge your partner to change just by being you. See what happens!

If you are holding on to hurt because someone left you, you still have to learn what your lesson is. Maybe it was like the rock story and you have just let yourself stay on the bottom. Now it is time to find and be you. Break your rock and plant your seed – see who else is in your garden!

Maybe it's not always about trying to fix something broken. Maybe it's about starting over and creating something better.

UNKNOWN

HELP PEOPLE UNDERSTAND YOU

Once you begin to understand yourself you can then invite others in your life to help you continue working on what your life lessons are. Invite them, without any fear, to get to know you, to help you know you. We are, after all, here to help each other not destroy each other. Remember how good it feels to spend time with a happy person, a person who loves life and loves themselves. We all truly want this for each other.

CLIENT EXAMPLE
Rebecca's issue is security or rather allowing herself to feel secure. This is a big life lesson for her. An only child, she came from a womb where an elder child had been terminated and she has felt very insecure for a very long time in all aspects of her life. She focuses on doing everything to make people like her, changing who she is in different groups and situations. Her focus is so much on what others think of her that it leaves her feeling insecure all the time. She is not free to like who she is, is too afraid to be who she is, and doesn't believe others will like her. This has proven to be a big problem in her relationships where she is very insecure and unconsciously always focusing on it. She struggles if her

boyfriend goes out without her, or has other friends that are women and then struggles even more to socialise with his friends because she believes they don't like her. This was the case in her last relationship and they separated because of this. This was the pattern in all of her relationships so far. In fact she had even had partners who had cheated on her (which proves that insecurity is certainly one of her life lessons), because she was attracting reasons to feel insecure all the time.

Her boyfriend missed her and they were talking about getting back together. She came to me asking for help. We discussed her life so far and that her insecurity was something to embrace and love about herself. We did some work on undoing her belief systems to free her from her no-choice reaction to situations and made a plan for her to work on.

She decided on a mantra she could say every day to remind her to keep focused on the positive side – I am safe and loved. When she felt insecure she could say this to remind herself it was now her choice. She could say this especially when they were out or when he was talking to other girls. She had the power to feel safe and secure – it was her choice.

At the same time as working on this she needed to help her boyfriend understand what she was working on. She needed to go through with him what didn't work for her. Understanding herself and helping him understand her would empower them both. They talked about her insecurity when other girls talked to him or when he went out with friends, etc. What he did was never the issue. Her feeling insecure was not his responsibility to make better for her. If he stopped talking to other girls and seeing his friends, I promise you she would find something else to feel insecure about, and he would feel trapped, he would have stopped himself from being his true self and ultimately both of them would be unhappy. Instead of making a list of what he could and couldn't do, she got the opportunity to explain to him something she now understood about herself. He gets the opportunity to remind her that he loves her and to help her on her journey. She got to explain, "So I am working on my feeling insecure and I am going to do these things when that feeling comes up for me." Now when they are out he can come up to her every now and again and whisper into her ear, "I am safe and loved." He gets to quite simply remind her to love herself first. This way, instead of focusing on what went wrong and instead of blaming each other for giving their power away and hoping the other one makes it better for them, they take responsibility for their own happiness and growth and bring a plan to the table. A plan to help each other so they can both understand their issues and work on plans to help each other empower themselves and their relationship.

There is no failure except in no longer trying.

ELBERT HUBBARD

UNDERSTAND THEM

The secret of a great relationship is not only to understand yourself but to also take the time to understand them

When we start to listen to our souls we also need to be aware of other people's souls – our parents, our kids, our partners and our friends. To get the most out of life, to be able to see the bigger picture, to be able to have peace, we need to also take the time to understand others. We need to find out what their souls are really saying.

There are hints in every aspect of our lives. Most people do what they need, a nurse will be in need of nurturing, a teacher may need to be listened to, a police officer may need to feel in control. If you can imagine how someone feels by doing what they do in their job then this can give you a big insight into them, their past and what they are actually trying to feel and learn. It's a big hint.

They are souls too. They also have an Earth body, a spiritual past and a genetic past – no wonder it gets hard sometimes!

Their bodies will also remember every single thing that has happened to them from the moment they were conceived. They formed patterns of how to deal with things, both physically, mentally, and emotionally. They made their own belief systems that are built from the time they were born until they were around seven. These belief systems will then influence how they react to things for the rest of their lives and what they attract into their lives. We need to understand their experiences so that we can empower ourselves and understand their 'whys' as in why do they do that or why do they react that way, or why have they attracted that to their life.

When you are dealing with other people, try to work out what their soul is saying, what the real feeling is. The words they give you *are not* what their soul is saying. Their soul, deep down, might be saying, I don't feel safe or I don't trust or I am scared of you leaving – I don't believe I am loveable. People use words and actions all the time to distract themselves from what they are trying to learn but if we are aware we can listen to what is underneath what their soul is saying. I promise you, their soul already knows the answer, but souls can't work it out by themselves on Earth. There are too many different layers when we add soul, spiritual past, genetic past and Earth experience! That is why we are all here together, why we are in each other's lives – to help each other work it out. We can't help if we don't turn our ladder sideways. We can't help if we continue to stay in Earth emotions of guilt, judgment, inadequacy, etc, and we can't help unless we understand ourselves. In fact, the only way to help anyone is to be truly yourself, to find your peace, to love who you are and to be who you were meant to be by embracing everything about you.

By having the courage to be yourself, you will inspire other people to change, to let go of all the 'Earth rules' to be their true selves. People want to feel peace and we can't give that to anyone, they have to find their own.

When trying to help each other focus on the feelings, is it of having no power, being inadequate, etc.? Once you are aware of it you can work through it together – you can both take your power back. You can both own your own feelings and by helping to give each other an insight into who you really are, you can understand you better, and they can understand you better, and then how you react to each other will change.

Often the way we think things are is not what is actually going on with the other person. We draw on our life experience and come to an assumption.

CLIENT EXAMPLE

I had a little prep boy come to see me. He was emotionally distraught every time his mum dropped him off at school. Both his mum and I assumed he was scared to go to school and felt very insecure without her. During his balance we discovered that his reason for tears was that he had taken on the role of protecting his mum and he was so worried about what she would do without him. We traced this back to when she was sick and he was a baby and did some work to clear it. His mum and he then went shopping and he bought a teddy bear for her handbag so that the teddy bear would look after her while he was at school. He went to school tear free from then on.

It's always a good idea when dealing with children (or anyone else for that matter) to ask what they think we have said. What happens is we tell them something and then they interpret it. What we say and what they hear can often be two different things. They can only understand things from their life experience. Sometimes it can be interesting when they repeat back to us what it is they think they have heard. This is a great habit to get into with all important conversations.

The fastest way to stop a mum is to get sick. When children get sick, mums will often stop the business of their lives, even take time off work, and nurture their child until they are back to health. Physically, mentally, emotionally and spiritually we remember this. So when we feel unloved or in desperate need of being nurtured we get sick. If children miss you they will get sick!

PERSONAL EXAMPLE

Christmas week is a really busy week for me. I had worked 90 hours and finished Christmas Eve knowing I had so much to do before Christmas Day. When I got home my daughter, aged nine at the time, was lying on the couch with a temperature of 39 and a headache and sore throat. I sat down and wrapped her in my arms and said to both her and her soul, "I understand, I am here now. I have a month off work to love you, to play with you, to have fun with you. You do not need to be sick to get my attention." Her throat was sore because she was unable to tell me her feelings. She was fine by the morning. She just needed reminding that she didn't have to be sick to get my attention.

When we are trying to help people through difficult

emotions we can be really inadequate. We don't like watching people in pain so we try to use our words to make it better. There are some interesting examples of this. If a grandparent dies, someone might say to you, "At least they had a good innings!" or "Maybe it was good they died peacefully." When people separate they might say, "We didn't like them anyway," or if a child is bullied we say "just ignore them". We say all of these words because we feel inadequate. We want them to feel better, to be back to their normal selves so we try to help them with very inadequate words.

Try putting your arms around someone and saying, "I will just hug you while you cry, and I can hug you as long as you need to cry!" It's okay, just feel it.

Children can teach us a lot. Healing our inner child can be done very quickly through spending time with kids and playing their games, like colouring, Play dough and cubby houses. It helps us to remember to keep things simple. Creativity can actually take a lot of stress away. We were all children once. We all still have that child in us. Our child in us needs to be loved, nurtured and acknowledged. Don't be afraid to embrace this.

Clearing things with children is often much easier and much quicker. The older we get the more time and life experience we have to suppress things, to misinterpret things and to create layered belief systems where we keep repeating the same cycle. We are like puzzles, we need to find lots of pieces before we can begin to get an idea of what our picture looks like. If it takes time to work yourself out and to see progress, don't be discouraged, you are further along than you were yesterday. You have all the time you need to work yourself out. Since you were born you have been sent many things that help to keep you on your path. That won't end. In fact you may be quite amazed by how much you will be able to see it now. Everything in your life is a message to you.

If we could look into each others hearts and understand the unique challenges each of us faces, I think we would treat each other much more gently, with more love, patience, tolerance and care.

MARVIN J ASHTON

Never discourage anyone who makes continual progress no matter how slow.

UNKNOWN

CHALLENGE EACH OTHER

We are in each other's lives to help each other. How many times do we hear people say, "Oh they are stuck in their ways." Whether it is our parents, our grandparents, the lady up the road, our children, other family members, anyone we come in contact with.

Why are people stuck in their ways? We don't stand in our truth, especially with the people we love.

Why? Due to fear, because we are afraid of confrontation, because we don't want them to feel bad, because we don't want to upset them, because we don't want to cause a rift in our family, because we are scared they might leave. Sometimes we even turn not confronting people into helping them. We make excuses for them, we support their behaviour, we actually help them be distracted by life and not listen to their souls. We help people stay in the same patterns.

Why? It is all about us and our issues. We need to be aware of this.

CLIENT EXAMPLE
Belinda is worried about her sister who struggles in life and seems to have no power. She is a recluse to the point she

now won't let anyone come into her messy house anymore. Belinda is very spiritual and helps people a lot but when it comes to her sister she never challenges her because she knows she won't change – she doesn't get this stuff. So what actually happens is that when she sees her sister she changes herself to be in her sister's world. She doesn't visit her house because she doesn't want to upset her.

It's like we forget the most important thing, that they are souls who never stop trying to learn their soul journey – we give up because we want to keep Earth peace and pretend happy families. Why do we hate getting together for Christmas so much? It is because no one ever stands in their truth, we just keep letting our family members continue on, in their own bullshit with no challenges because we are scared and don't want to rock the boat. We say they won't listen, they are stuck in their ways, all the time watching them become sick, etc. Well, they are souls above and beyond anything else and if they are still alive on Earth then they are still trying and you need to honour their soul and stand in your truth and be you.

When you challenge someone you are just being your soul. You are not taking on responsibility for that person. You are not trying to change them. Especially with family, have a think about what their issue or lesson might be. Have a look at what they have attracted into their life and their patterns. Be honest with yourself and allow your soul to speak. Speak with love and peace and don't react. It's like when you say how you feel, it is a present for them. Give it to them without holding onto the outcome or their reaction. All you are doing is presenting a creative learning opportunity for them, it's up to them to keep it or not.

One of my favourite girlfriends is completely opposite to me and I love her dearly. We are both exactly who we are with each other. She will say she hurt her ankle. I will say it's because you are struggling moving forward with something. She will say maybe it's because I tripped on a rock. She will say her whole family is sick with a cold. I will say that is a lot of unsaid emotion. She will say it's because a virus came and visited their house. We both laugh and hug each other. We aren't trying to change the other person or the way they think. Neither of us is taking responsibility to fix each other and no raffle tickets are ever exchanged (we don't try to make the other person feel something), we are both just being our trueselves.

Always continue the climb. It is possible for you to do whatever you choose if you first get to know who you are and are willing to work with a power that is greater than ourselves to do it.

ELLA WHEELER WILCOX

CONCLUSION

I still yell at my children, I still try to manipulate my husband, I can still be manipulated by other people. I am, after all, a soul in an Earth body with a spiritual past, a genetic past and all my life experiences.

I am, however, learning to love myself. When I turn my ladder sideways, when I bake my own cake, when I really listen to my soul and to what other people's souls are trying to say, when I understand and embrace my lessons, when I water my own garden, when I hug 'n' rock, when I stop taking raffle tickets or giving them out, when I embrace wholeheartedly how I feel, when I give people back their own responsibility, when I work out how I can feel safe and when I trust with no outcome, then I have the answer. I have peace. I love unconditionally who I am. Every day I try to do this I get better at it.

I invite you to do the same.

Workshops on *Soul Talk Earth Walk* are available through www.melryan100percentyou.com.

GLOSSARY

Affirmation – A self-affirming positive statement.

Aura – The energy field around a person's physical body.

Balance – A kinesiology treatment session.

Balloon Theory – The amount of people you are trying to keep happy at the same time.

Bake Your Cake – The ability to love who you are without affirmation from anyone else.

Being – Who you are meant to be, without influence from anyone else.

Belief System – Thought patterns developed that influence us every day.

Blame – A way to stay stuck in something.

Breakdown – When someone is in urgent need of breaking their life down to a manageable level.

Change – The essence of life and guaranteed to happen.

Communication – The ability to really listen and express your true self.

Dad Earth – A dad who tries to make everything in his child's life perfect.

Dad Soul – A dad who can see the bigger picture for his child, and trust his child's higher self

Date Yourself – The perfect way to get to know yourself.

Emotion Earth – Emotions that block, sabotage and teach us, you can only experience these on Earth.

Emotion Soul – Emotions that allow us to rejoice in ourselves, are available and recommended for us to feel on Earth.

Emotional Patterning – Incorporating past emotional memories.

Expectations – Assumptions that are imposed upon us.

Expectations Movable – No matter what you get done you still like yourself.

Feelings – Are like Lego, they build up unless you understand and move them. They are learning opportunities.

Forgiveness – Something you have found peace in.

Genetic History – A link back to our past generations both DNA, emotional and spiritual.

Guilt – A creative learning opportunity for all parties involved.

Holiday – A Feeling.

Hug 'n' Rock – A concept of parenting where we don't interfere.

Ladder – How we see ourselves and where we fit in, in life.

Ladder Sideways – Everyone is equal.

Magic Wand – A wonderful hint of what is really going on with a person.

Mum Earth – A mum who tries to make everything in her child's life perfect.

Mum Soul – A mum who can see the bigger picture for her child, and trust her child's higher self.

Mercury Theory – Together we are one.

Pain – An emotion.

Pedestal – Putting expectations on someone else.

Person Free – A person who needs to feel free – this feeling influences their life.

Person Safe – A person who needs to feel safe – this feeling influences their life.

Pool Earth – Where most people swim. Full of limitations to being who you are meant to be.

Pool Soul – Where we are meant to be. Allows us to feel like we are in heaven, on Earth.

Power Bubble – Your essence. Your ability to feel self-empowered.

Power Bubble Battle – Losing and taking power from others so you can try to keep your ability to feel self-empowered.

Raffle Tickets – Trying to invoke a feeling in someone else.

Reality – There is a much bigger picture.

Responsibility – It is all yours.

Rock – It has your beautiful seed inside. If you are a rock then you are allowing yourself to be squashed.

Stand in your Power – Knowing what is right for you and not letting Earth rules of feelings influence you otherwise.

Stand in your Truth – There are no lies here, no matter how hard it is.

Soul Group – A group of souls they help make sure you are learning your soul lessons.

Soul Lessons – Why we are here. To learn.

Soul Mate – Is you.

Themes – Continually reoccurring emotions and life patterns that are trying to teach you something.

Treat – Something you do for yourself that makes you feel loved by you.

Treat Food – Something healthy, that makes your body feel wonderful and tastes delicious.

Trust Earth – Something that always gets damaged.

Trust Universal – The ability to trust with no outcome in mind. Having an awareness of a much bigger picture and that there is a reason for everything.

Unconditional Love – Pure.

Water your own Garden – Looking after yourself and enjoying it.

What the point is – To listen to our souls and our bodies, to understand and to learn.

Worrying – A waste of energy.

REFERENCES

The Five People You Meet In Heaven, Mitch Albom, 98
You Can Heal Your Life, Louise L. Hay, 123
The Body Is The Barometer Of The Soul, Annette Noontilare, 123
Metaphysical Anatomy, Evette Rose, 123
The Crystal Children, Doreen Virtue, 126
The Celestine Prophecies, James Redfern, 176

AFFIRMATIONS

A few examples of affirmations I set people for homework regularly:
I am being my own being.
I allow me to be me.
I allow me to be who my soul wants to be.
I am here 100% in present time.
I am safe.
I allow myself to feel safe.
I allow myself to feel free.
I allow myself to look after me.
I trust in a bigger picture.
I am worthy.
I allow myself to be powerful
There is time for everything I want to do.
I choose to.
I am exactly where I am meant to be physically, emotionally, mentally and spiritually.

www.ingramcontent.com/pod-product-compliance
Lightning Source LLC
Chambersburg PA
CBHW071857290426
44110CB00013B/1185